Editor
Walter Kelly

Editorial Project Manager
Ina Massler Levin, M.A.

Editor in Chief
Sharon Coan, M.S. Ed.

Illustrator
Chandler Sinnott

Cover Artist
Agi Palinay

Art Coordinator
Denice Adorno

Creative Director
Elayne Roberts

Imaging
Alfred Lau

Product Manager
Phil Garcia

Publishers
Rachelle Cracchiolo, M.S. Ed.
Mary Dupuy Smith, M.S. Ed.

How t
Your Classroom

Author

Sheri Mabry Bestor, M.A.

Teacher Created Materials, Inc.
6421 Industry Way
·   Westminster, CA 92683
www.teachercreated.com
ISBN-1-57690-513-6
©1999 Teacher Created Materials, Inc.
Made in U.S.A.

Table of Contents

Table of Contents *(cont.)*

Introduction

Congratulations! You have taken your first step toward becoming a more organized, productive, and effective teacher. By reading and adopting the methods in *How to Organize Your Classroom,* you will find that the seemingly endless hours spent grading, recordkeeping, communicating with parents, attending curriculum and staff meetings, even sorting through the piles of mail will take less time and leave you with more time to teach.

Student Benefits

Actually, the prime benefits of a well-organized classroom will accrue to your students. Your organization and procedures (or lack thereof) are, after all, ever-present reminders to the children of how to behave, how to conduct their business, and how best to be effective without discord in a group. Respect for others, consideration, efficiency, pride of accomplishment, security in knowing what, how, when, and where to do something—all these positive elements are the hallmarks and characteristics of students who learn in well-organized classrooms. Children like a predictable, safe, and orderly environment—and they like going to a school that provides that environment. For these reasons alone, it behooves any teacher to pay close attention to good organization.

Teacher Benefits

Aside from the benefits to students, good organization brings powerful help to the teacher. In fact, it can be truthfully said that the first "aide" any teacher has is his or her ability to organize the classroom well.

The immediate benefits of a well-organized classroom to the teacher are clear—less wasted time and therefore more efficiency. Not so immediately apparent, perhaps, are the following very significant elements:

- reduced teacher fatigue
- improved parent-teacher relations
- increased enthusiasm for professional growth
- improved student-teacher relations
- increased job satisfaction
- increased student academic progress

This manual will explain how to use each of the masters in the back of the book, as well as give you ideas and strategies to help you to become more organized. Also included in this section is a supplemental list of forms useful in many teaching situations. Read through them and adapt the ideas to fit your style.

With the help of this book and a little effort, you will reduce stress and find yourself becoming an organized, efficient, and, therefore, a more effective teacher!

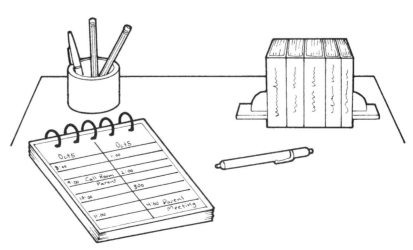

4

Setting Up Your Classroom

The space, materials, furniture, manipulatives, resources, games, and number of students found in a classroom will vary from one classroom to the next. However, the following hints will make your classroom conducive to effective organization. These ideas will help keep your classroom in order, save you time, and allow you to become the most effective teacher possible.

Teacher's Desk

Before you place the teacher's desk in your room, you need to determine how you will be using it during the school year; it can be a working area for helping students, correcting papers, and working on lesson plans or simply a place to store materials. If your desk is primarily a place to store supplies, put it in a corner out of the way, far from students and movement. If possible, remove it from your room altogether. There are more effective storage bins that take up less space than desks.

If your desk is to become a working area, it must be placed where it is readily accessible to you and your students; in other words, don't have it hidden behind bookshelves or within a maze of resource materials. Your desk must be set so that you can see the entire room and all of the students just by glancing up. You should also have a view of the emergency exit door. Placing the desk diagonally along an outside wall allows you to view the entire classroom while simultaneously providing space behind it for your chair and filing cabinets. Suggestions for classroom setup can be found in the Master Copies section (pages 87–89) of this resource book.

Students' Desks

Students' desks should be arranged in accordance to the grade level as well as your teaching philosophy. Younger grade levels allow the desks to be set closer together, while older grade levels need more space. Teaching with cooperative groups permits you to cluster the desks in sets of three or four. Depending upon your teaching style, you might prefer setting your desks in straight rows or groups of two. Variations of seating charts can be found in the Master Copies section (pages 78–80). Keep in mind that students must be able to see you and any visuals if you plan on using a chalkboard, flannelboard, or eraser board. No desks should be hidden from view in any way. Also, if your school requires students to place their chairs on top of their desks at the end of the day, make sure that you allow enough room between desks to be able to put the chairs up easily. When setting up the desks, imagine that students are sitting in their chairs. Make sure there is enough room for the students to sit comfortably. Think about the size of the student in relation to the size of his or her desk, as well as the sizes of the desks you place next to each other. A very short desk next to a very tall desk may result in one banging into the other when they are opened. Avoiding small annoyances like these eliminates undue stress and allows for a more orderly classroom.

Setting Up Your Classroom (cont.)

Teacher's Manuals

Determining where you place your supply of teacher's manuals will depend on how much you rely on the manuals. If you rely on them often, then they should be placed wherever you use them the most. You might obtain two copies, keep one set where you meet with the students or where you teach from, and keep the other set on your desk to use for correcting students' work or planning new lessons. Place tabs in the manuals so that you may quickly and easily refer to the pages where you are working. Label each with a color-coded bookmark to help you select the current resource quickly and readily.

Library

You will need to keep the free-reading resources for your students easily accessible to them. You might use shelves up against a wall or, even better, standing out in the open so that you might use both sides. (Make sure the shelves are sturdy and won't tip!) Alphabetize your books so that students practice library skills when searching for books as well as when replacing them. As divisions for the books, use large tag tabs with the letters clearly marked. You might also want to arrange the books by subject to help students make their selections.

Group Space

Arrange an area where students can sit on the floor in a large group to meet with you. This is where you would read stories to the class, have group discussions, do experiments, etc. The area should be near the chalkboard or eraser board with chalk or markers always available. Also have paper, pens, teacher resource materials, and student copies of materials nearby. The chapter book you are reading to the kids, mind puzzlers, seating charts, and grade books might all be resources you will find useful at this spot. It would be ideal to have this area near a window for the benefits of natural light and fresh air.

Colored Carpet Samples

Depending upon the age of the students, you may wish to use colored carpet samples in your classroom. You can place them in certain areas, depending upon where you'd like the students to sit. If they are to be reading silently, spread the samples around the room and have each student choose the one he or she would like. If they are to be sitting with partners, place the carpet samples in twos throughout the room. It is ideal to have the carpet samples set on the floor before the students come into the room. When they enter, they know they are to go directly to a carpet sample and get to the task—free reading, practicing with flashcards, going over a script, etc. This is an excellent method for starting out the class with DEAR (Drop Everything and Read). Students will quietly be getting to work while selected students are handing back papers, and you have a chance to meet with students who were absent the day before.

Drop Everything And Read

Setting Up Your Classroom (cont.)

Supplies

Classroom supplies are always a necessity. Some schools require students to come to class with their own supplies or have them stored in their desks. It is beneficial for teachers to also have a supply of office materials for students to use. Pencils with your name taped on them, pens with your initials taped on them, erasers, paper clips, scissors, and a stapler (depending upon the age of the students) might be placed in a basket to be used by your students. Glue for student use can be placed in another basket in the room.

Chalkboard

Divide your chalkboard according to your lesson plans. You might have an area to post the day's schedule and date. Another area might be used to post the reading lessons. The next area might be designated for math figuring. And yet another may be for penmanship. You can divide the chalkboard with colored rubber tape (don't use masking tape because it won't come off very easily). Then consistently use a different color of chalk in each area of the board. For example, always write the reading lessons in blue chalk, math in yellow, etc.

Besides having a supply of white and colored chalk and clean erasers, you might also want to purchase or make board cups. These are simple plastic cups with magnetic strips attached. Place these on the board and keep pens, markers, a pair of scissors, and pencils in them for use if your large group area is near the chalkboard. You can demonstrate art projects, jot down notes, and edit lesson plans from your large group teaching spot by using these materials which are stored on your chalkboard. You may want to make sure the students know that these materials are teacher materials and not to be used by students. You may use strong magnetic tape to keep a clipboard with notepaper attached to the chalkboard as well.

You may also have a portable chalkboard. This can be used as a versatile divider or a two-sided resource—chalkboard on one side, bulletin board on the other. Either way, place this portable chalkboard/bulletin board where the students can see it from their seats, but where it does not block the view to the main chalkboard or to your desk.

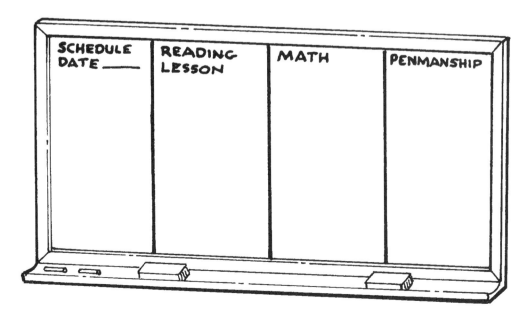

Setting Up Your Classroom (cont.)

Paper

Have a supply of drawing and writing paper labeled for your students' use. You can use cardboard boxes placed sideways to hold the paper in organized piles.

Bulletin Boards

Have bulletin boards available for seasonal projects as well as extra-credit projects and a special section called "Student Choices." Student Choices will be an area designated for students to post any project or piece of writing of which they are particularly proud. The areas can be divided by children's last names (for example, an area for A–L) or specific academic groups so that when students place their work on the board, they know which area to use. This ensures that everyone always has a spot to put his or her work, and, with a glance, you can keep track of the posted work.

Special Room Organization Tips

- *Out and In Bins:* Have one area on your desk that is for projects or assignments kids hand in, and another for those papers that have been corrected and need to be handed back. If you teach several subjects, you will need to have an in and out box for each class. You might use stackable metal or plastic baskets. Let the students know about these in and out boxes on the first day of school. The students should be taught to hand their things in when they are completed. You will take that pile at the end of the day, correct the papers, and put them into the out bin by the 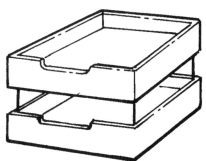 next morning. As soon as students arrive in class, the first student is allowed to come to the out bin and distribute those papers while the other kids are settling into their seats. Kids love this "duty." It also saves valuable time collecting or handing out papers during the middle of class.

- *No Name:* Have a large clip to hold all of the students' work that doesn't have a name. When papers are being handed out, students who do not receive theirs will know to check the "no name" clip to find their missing papers. This saves you from taking the time to go through each nameless piece, holding it up in class, and waiting for someone to claim it.

- *Mailboxes:* You may use one or two cardboard shoe dividers that you can buy in your local department store for your students' mail. In these mailboxes, place papers to go home, special notes to kids, finished papers, and homework that students miss when they are absent. Label each cube with a child's name, using laminated colored labels and permanent markers. When you need to reuse the labels the following year, use hair spray on them and the marker ink can be wiped off. Another suggestion is to put a small mailbox on your desk for students to reach you if they need to jot you a note or have a concern or a question.

- *Coat Hangers:* You may want to assign your students coat hangers in alphabetical order by their last names. This will help you at the end of the day by allowing you to take just a glance to determine who left a hat, coat, backpack, etc.

Setting Up Your Classroom *(cont.)*

Special Room Organization Tips *(cont.)*

- *Lunch Tickets:* Instead of allowing your students to keep their tickets in their desks where they can easily be lost, create a pocket poster with the names on them for students to store their own tickets in. Place it at a height in your room easily accessible by each student. Be sure it is on a wall that is away from where the students line up so that they don't have to push through a line to retrieve their lunch tickets.

- *Music:* Depending upon the rules in your school and whether you share a classroom with other teachers, you may want to have a stereo in the room for quiet music. This can be used as a reward at times or when students are working on art or other projects. The stereo might be placed either behind your desk—thus, off limits to students—or where students can access it, depending upon your preference.

- *Pencil Sharpener:* Keep this away from all students' desks and your desk, if possible, so that the sound of grinding won't disturb those who are working.

Technology

Chances are that you won't have much choice about where to place computers or tape recorders in your room; you will need to place them where the outlets are and where students won't trip over the cords. However, give some consideration to the angle at which you place the computers. Will the students working at the computer be able to see the board that you want them to reference? Are the computers located far enough away from individual desks so as not to disturb those working at their desks? The software itself should be well labeled and located near the computers.

When reviewing the Classroom Maps in the Master Copies section (pages 87–89) at the back of this reference book, it is suggested that you use parts of each of the various suggestions to set up a classroom that best fits your teaching style.

Summary

It is essential that you spend time and thought as to how you arrange your classroom. If placed strategically, furniture, materials, resources, student desks, even the writing on the chalkboard will enhance your teaching by providing an organized and pleasant environment.

Creating Order in the Classroom

Being organized is more than having your papers filed correctly and your work done on time. It means having an organized system at work in your environment—one that is time efficient, stress-free, and manageable. Creating order in the classroom will not only help you to become a more organized instructor, it will instill in the students valuable skills as well.

Rules

It is important that on the first day of school you have a class discussion to establish the ground rules with your students. One method is to come up with the rules that you feel are important and write them on a chart prior to this group discussion. Keep this chart posted in the classroom at all times throughout the year. It is unfair to have expectations for students that they are unaware of. The rules themselves will vary from classroom to classroom, depending upon the grade level, your teaching philosophy, the school's setup, and other criteria. However, the following are examples of some basic rules that will most likely apply to your situation:

Classroom Rules

1. Treat everyone with respect.

2. Walk. (Don't run inside.)

3. Use "inside" voices.

4. Raise your hand.

The rules should be simple and easy to follow, and there should not be too many. "Treat everyone with respect," for example, covers many other specific behaviors—don't hit, talk back, yell at others, push, talk behind others' backs, interrupt, etc. When discussing the list of rules, be sure to cover all the meanings for each rule.

Another method when presenting the idea of classroom rules is to formulate your list of rules, but NOT share them with the class. Rather, present a blank poster and have the students brainstorm a list of rules. Once the students have come up with a whole list, go over it together and edit to find the five or ten most important rules. Write them on the poster. If the students fail to come up with any rules that you feel are important to include, try to guide them to mention the rules you have in mind. Giving the students ownership in the rules makes it more likely that they will remember and follow them, thus promoting not only a safer, more organized environment, but a happier one as well.

Creating Order in the Classroom *(cont.)*

Routines

It is extremely beneficial to develop routines. This provides stability for students and allows the classroom to run smoothly. Some ideas of areas in which to develop routines are the following:

Lining Up

Have a general rule on how students line up. Although you don't want such a strict, organized environment that kids become uptight, it is helpful to allow students the benefit of organized routines, such as how to line up for certain events. The following ideas may help avoid running to get into line and/or pushing and arguing as to "who is first." (As you know, these conflicts seem to occur most frequently with the younger students.)

- When the students line up, the first one who is quiet can be the leader. (Being the "first" is important for the younger kids.)

- The first one who is finished with his or her tasks or is cleaned up first is able to line up first, the next will be second, and so on.

- The person whose birthday it is may be the line leader.

- Teach the students how to line up in alphabetical order according to their last names. This will not only focus on a language arts skill, it will allow the teacher in the next class to take attendance more efficiently. When the students enter the next classroom, the teacher can zip down the class roster list, and attendance will take half the time. Moreover, students will learn alphabetical order and who they should be standing next to. When that person is absent, they can alert the teacher upon entering the classroom. Use this method on field trips, as well, to keep track of the students.

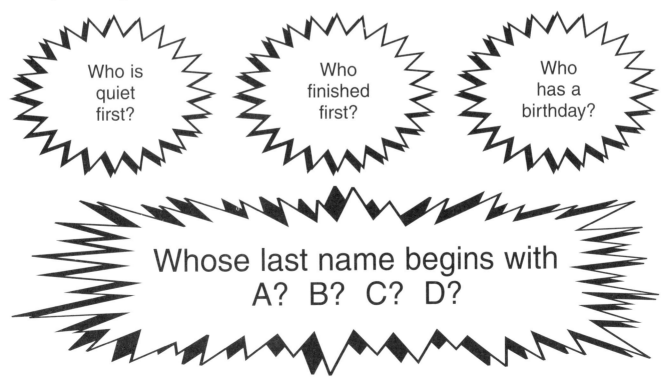

Creating Order in the Classroom (cont.)

Routines (cont.)

Lunch Count

School lunch is offered at almost all schools, but the procedure varies as to determining on a daily basis who will be participating in the school lunch program. You will need to adopt a system that is best for your situation, using the following ideas to help:

- When students walk into the room in the morning, have them learn to put a check or mark by their name on a list if they want school lunch. Those students who are in need of a free lunch will be able to remain anonymous by participating in this procedure.

- Have them stand up in the morning, and you count the number of students who want school lunch.

- Provide the students with a magnetic "S" in their desks. Those who want school lunch for the day may put their "S" on the chalkboard in the designated spot. One child is in charge of counting the "S's" and giving you the final count.

Hand Washing

For health reasons, students should always wash their hands before they eat lunch or any snack. To make the procedure run more efficiently, explain how the routine will work. Students will line up behind the sink. The one whose turn it is gets his or her hands wet, applies ONE squirt of soap (liquid soap is less messy and more sanitary than bar soap), rinses again, and uses TWO pumps of the paper towels. For the tear type or individual dispensers, one piece of paper towel will do. Leave water on so that that next child can come right up and begin his or her turn. Have the trash bucket near the sink so that as they leave they can toss the paper towel directly into the bucket.

Creating Order in the Classroom *(cont.)*

Routines *(cont.)*

Bathroom Use

Interrupting your reading lesson several times within the class period for various students to ask permission to use the bathroom is not only an inefficient use of time, but it is also frustrating for the students you are working with and awkward for the students asking. Adopt one of the following systems for your classroom:

- *Pass System:* Have a "boy's pass" and a "girl's pass" that hang on the wall. If a student needs to use the bathroom, he or she takes the appropriate pass and returns it to the hook when re-entering the room.

- *Stop/Go Sign System:* When the "go" is displayed on the chalkboard, a student may go up to the board, turn the sign to "stop," and then go to the bathroom. When that person returns, he or she needs to turn the sign back to "go."

- *Sign-Out System:* Have the students sign their names on a fixed area of the chalkboard when they need to go to the bathroom. If someone's name is already there, the student must wait until that person returns and erases his or her name.

- *Buddy System:* For those students who are unable to travel through the school on their own, develop a buddy system. Assign two students to each other who you know will be able to handle walking to the bathroom together, and allow them to leave the room as a pair. Keep a record of who you paired together. Have them sign out when they leave the room.

Whatever system you adopt should keep the kids from going to the bathroom in large groups, as well as allowing you to know who or how many are out of the room and where. This is necessary not only for academic reasons but also in the event of a natural disaster or emergencies.

Absence and Missed Assignments

The methods you use with absentees depend upon the age level you are working with and how much responsibility you want to give to the students. Adopt one of the following to fit your classroom needs:

- You may have the students notify you if they have been absent; make them responsible for asking you for the missed work. Keep some time free each day to meet with students who need extra help because of missed class time.

- Each day, check who is absent, and put the absent student's name at the top of any of the papers you are handing out. Then drop those papers into the "out" bin. The next day the papers will be passed out to the students who were absent. You may even jot notes at the tops, such as "See me." The students will then approach you when they receive the paperwork.

Creating Order in the Classroom (cont.)

Routines (cont.)

Handing in Work

Simply devise an "in" and "out" system. It works best if you have an "in" box for each subject you teach. Instruct the students that when they have completed their work, they are to place it in the proper "in" box. When you have the time, you will be able to take the papers from the "in" box, correct them, record comments and grades, and place them into the "out" bin to be handed out the next time that class meets.

If all the students are completing the work at the same time (as in the case of a spelling test, for example) collect the papers in ABC order by calling out the letters of the alphabet. When the students hear the letter that begins their last name, they will bring their papers up to you. This will allow you to be able to record the grades, once you have corrected them, just by going through the papers in the order that you had collected them and recording the marks in your grade book. At the same time, of course, you are reinforcing your instruction on alphabetical order.

No Name

Obtain a magnetic clip to attach to your metal desk or to the chalkboard in a designated location. Label it "No Name." When you come upon a paper that does not have a student's name on it, place it in the "No Name" clip. When all of the other students receive their work, the student who doesn't receive his or hers will go check the "No Name" clip. Instruct the student to hand in the paper again with a name on it so that you can record the grade.

Questions

Students will, of course, need to raise their hands when they are gathered in a group and have questions or comments. However, there may be times when students would like to ask you something without their peers hearing them. It may be difficult during the day for them to find you alone to be able to air their concerns. So it benefits every student for you to have available a personal mailbox for questions they don't feel comfortable asking in front of the class. This may be a mini mailbox purchased at an office supply store, or it may be one you create. Either way, at the beginning of the year explain its use. Keep the mini-mailbox on your desk. Allow students to put comments, questions, or concerns on paper and "mail" them to you. When you see the flag up, retrieve your mail. Always make sure to respond in a timely manner to the student. Also, record any concerns under "Student Information." (See Student Information/Parent Communications Book on pages 44 and 45.) Although this may not seem like a routine that aids in organization, again, eliminating stress in students creates a more comfortable and smoothly run environment.

Creating Order in the Classroom *(cont.)*

Routines *(cont.)*

Passing Out Notes

The endless letters and fliers that go home to students must be handled efficiently. Use one of the following methods to keep the distribution of these papers simple.

- Obtain a magnetic paper holder and stick it to the chalkboard. This may be a cardboard or plastic bin with strong magnetic tape glued to the back. The bin should allow 8.5" x 11" (22 cm x 28 cm) papers to fit within. Or, it may be a holder hung from a strong clip on the bulletin board. (Hanging this holder instead of placing it on a table or desk frees up table and desk space.) Put the papers in this holder anytime you receive any information to be handed out by the end of the day. The student acting as the weekly helper who is to hand out papers will check that holder when entering the classroom and hand the papers out immediately.

- Hand out the papers by distributing them into personal mailboxes made of shoe dividers you can purchase at local department stores. Again, this task of putting papers into the mailboxes may be assigned to an individual student, or you may leave time to accomplish this task (such as the last five minutes before the last recess ends) and do it yourself. You can also make your own mailbox system by using shoeboxes and cardboard dividers.

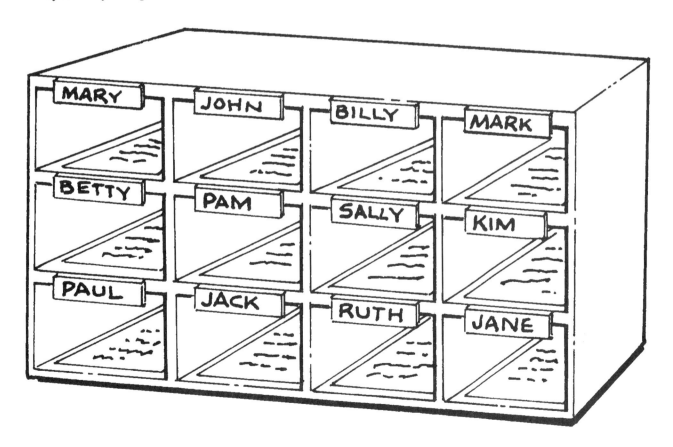

Creating Order in the Classroom (cont.)

Attendance

If your school does not have a system in place already, choose one of the following methods that will best fit your needs when taking attendance:

- Have students check their names off the attendance sheet upon entering the classroom.

- Have the first student who enters the room take attendance of the others who enter.

- Have students volunteer who is absent by noticing who is not present at the desks next to them.

- Place students' names on individual magnetic strips on the chalkboard. Have students take their names off the chalkboard every morning when they enter the room. The names that haven't been taken off the board belong to the students who are absent. Have the students replace their names at the end of the day or whenever they have to leave school early.

- If students put up their chairs on top of their desks at the end of the day, record whose chairs are still up the following morning after the students have arrived and are seated.

- Have students entering from another class line up in alphabetical order. Then take attendance as they come into the room.

Although it is beneficial to involve the students in the taking of attendance, remember that it is your responsibility to make sure the final count is accurate. Therefore, make sure you always check the final list.

Duties

Most students love having a duty to help out in the classroom. It makes them feel special and gives them a sense of ownership in their room. Make a "class helpers" chart and have the kids volunteer, pick names from a hat, or rotate the students so that they will all have an opportunity to do each task at some point during the year. Some of the tasks you may want done in the classroom are the following:

- *Passing Out Notes*: This student distributes the notes that need to go out, such as fliers and other informational newsletters. This child is responsible for making sure every student receives one.

- *Passing Out Papers*: This student is responsible for coming into the class and looking into the "out" bin. This student passes out the completed homework and puts the papers that don't have names into the "no name" clip. The papers of the students who are absent are put back into the "out" bin to distribute the next day.

- *Checking the Floor*: The student who is responsible for the floor makes sure that all of the scraps are picked up off the floor and thrown away at the end of the day.

- *Checking the Chairs*: This student will make sure all of the chairs are pushed into the desks. He or she is responsible at the end of the day for putting the chair on top of the desk for anyone who is absent. He or she is also responsible for taking the chair down for anyone who is absent the next morning—after the teacher records who is absent, of course.

Creating Order in the Classroom *(cont.)*

Duties *(cont.)*

- *Checking Computers*: This task involves making sure the disks are put away and that the computer and printer are turned off when not in use.

- *Checking Books*: This student straightens the classroom books and makes sure they remain in alphabetical order or whatever order they are to be in within your classroom.

- *Checking the Sink*: This person wipes up the sink after the last person washes his or her hands before lunch. He or she is also responsible for making sure soap and paper towels are available and alerting the teacher when the supply runs low. For those classrooms without carpet, students may also wipe the area of the floor near the sink with paper towels after students have completed washing their hands.

- *Checking Attendance*: This person helps with whatever system you adopt for taking attendance.

- *Checking Plants*: This person waters the plants on a weekly basis. If there are fish or other classroom pets, this student will be taught to properly and safely take care of them.

- *Checking Cleanup*: At the end of the day, this person helps to make sure the glue bottles are put away, the scissors are stored neatly, and the crayons and other art supplies are where they belong. This person is also instructed to encourage fellow classmates to clean up their areas.

- *Cleaning the Chalkboard*: At the end of the day, this person erases and washes the chalkboard and tray.

- *Posting the Date*: Every morning, this person will write the current date in the designated spot on the chalkboard.

- *Running Errands*: This student is the individual you call on to run errands for you. He or she will take notes to other teachers, travel to the school office to retrieve your mail, etc.

Class Helpers

Check Floor	Mary	Run Errands	Tran
Check Sink	John	Return Papers	Thuy
Check Chairs	Steve	Post Date	Victor
Check Plants	Andrea	Clean Board	Rafael

Creating Order in the Classroom (cont.)

Cleanup in the Classroom

Although there will be students whose task it is to maintain general order in the classroom, it is important to have an organized way to maintain cleanliness and order. Have designated spots for all items such as the following:

- glue
- pencils
- recycling bin
- paper
- scrap paper
- books
- scissors
- paper clips and other paper fasteners
- recess games

- crayons
- tissue
- garbage bin

- math manipulatives
- teacher resources
- computer programs
- paper towels

You might purchase some inexpensive plastic baskets or cardboard shoe-storage bins to hold some of the above items. Shelves should be labeled accordingly.

◆

Have a classroom map posted to allow students to help restore the order of the classroom.

◆

Use rubber tape (not masking tape!) on the floor to let the students know where their desks are to be. Simply mark where the front corners of the desk should be located on the floor. At the end of the day, all the students can take a few seconds to straighten their desks so that they are arranged in the format that they should be in.

◆

Put things back where you found them and encourage the students to do the same. Try to maintain a consistent general order in the classroom. If you are constantly rearranging things, it will be difficult for the students to notice when things are out of order.

◆

Make students aware of where things belong and why, how to use items, and classroom routines and rules. Let them know not only what tasks they are assigned to (it is helpful to let them partake in the assignment of these tasks) but also when and how often they are to perform them. Make sure you keep your area orderly and clean as well, as you are leading by example.

◆

Using some or all of the above hints will help create a more orderly and thus, a less stressful classroom environment for you and your students. The master copies in the back of the book (pages 87–89) will give you helpful ideas on how to develop classroom maps.

Teaching Students to Be Organized

Along with mastering academics and building social skills, students will benefit from gaining organizational skills. Being organized not only makes one more productive, it is a sought-after attribute in the job market. Although students will benefit from observing organized parents, teachers, and peers, it is important to teach them the strategies of organization as well.

Supplies and Folders

At the end of a school year, send home a supplies list for the following year or have it sent to all of the students' families before the first day of school. You, your grade level, your principal, or your team leader may generate this list. Items to possibly include are in the following list:

Needed Supplies

- five sharpened number 2 pencils (make certain to underline the number "2" because those pencil types are needed for all Scantron testing.)
- one box of tissue*
- one bottle of white, nontoxic glue* (or a gluestick, depending upon the grade level)
- one pair of scissors
- one ruler
- pens (depending upon the grade level)
- one package of lined college-rule paper* (depending upon the grade)
- five pocket folders (depending upon your needs): blue, red, orange, green, yellow
- two erasers
- one pencil box
- calculator (depending upon your school's resources as well as the age of the students)
- crayons
- markers (depending upon the grade level of the students)
- colored pencils
- academic calendars (dates from September through June)
- _____
- _____

These items* will be pooled together and shared throughout the year. With the contribution from each student, the supply should last until the end of the year.

Make sure to send out the list well in advance of the first day of school. Supplies at local office stores run out, and parents need time to locate the required materials.

Teaching Students to Be Organized (cont.)

Supplies and Folders (cont.)

On the first day of school, it is necessary to emphasize with the students the importance of taking good care of their supplies. Although the students are excited about their new supplies and are eager to treat them with respect and care, soon these same items will lose their "first day newness" and many will be tossed into desks, left behind, broken, or thrown away. Have parents label all personal items with the child's name and teacher's name or room number in permanent marker before the items are brought to school. This will save you valuable class time.

- Label, or have the students label, each folder for each class. Color-code them—for example, all red folders are to be used for reading classes, all blue folders are to be used for math classes, etc. This will not only help the teacher in organization, but it will enable the students to quickly gather supplies for the next class they will be attending.

- Teach the students how to arrange their supplies in their pencil boxes. Explain that they should always have sharpened pencils, keep their crayons neatly in the original box, etc. Have them keep two of everything in their boxes and keep the extras stored neatly in their desks. Have them make sure their pencil boxes have their names clearly marked on the outside.

- Label one of the folders "take home." Within the folder, label the pocket on the right side "to school" and label the left pocket "to home." Teach the students to place all unfinished homework and notes in the "to home" section and all finished work to be handed in and any notes to the teachers in the right pocket labeled "to school."

Calendar System

It is essential for students to begin using a calendar system to learn how to accomplish tasks on time and to consistently keep their appointments. Take some time on one of the first days of school to discuss using a calendar. Each student should have a calendar because it was an item listed on their supplies list, but undoubtedly the calendars will all be somewhat different. Show examples of different calendars and how to use each. Explain how to practice the habit of jotting down assignments the minute they are assigned. Emphasize indicating in the calendar when tasks are completed. Stress the importance of prioritizing tasks. Include suggestions for noting reminders on certain days, such as "science project due in three days, begin working on it." Periodically check students' calendars (with their permission) to see they are keeping up with their assignments and reminders. Once they learn to use calendars, they will recognize their value.

April						
SUN	MON	TUES	WED	THURS	FRI	SAT
				1	2	3
4	5	6 Science Project due	7	8	9	10
11	12	13	14	15	16	17
18	19	20	21	22 Reading Test	23	24
25	26	27	28	29	30	

Teaching Students to Be Organized (cont.)

Student Desks, Bins, or Lockers

Depending upon where students store their materials, have them learn how to organize and arrange their materials within the storage space. Teach them how to organize their folders and supplies that they will be taking to each class so that they can enter their storage space and quickly retrieve the materials without clumsy searching that messes up the materials.

Homework and Notes

Teach students to indicate in their calendars when homework is due. Encourage students to place homework assignments immediately in the proper place in their take-home folders. Teach the students about notes, as well. Have students indicate notes in their calendars (for example, "zoo permission slip due back by Friday").

Explain the importance of having a homework area at home—not only to do homework in but also to keep and store the homework—so that when the student leaves each morning, he or she can check the area to make sure the folder is remembered. Parents and students may use this area to store notes from school, homework that needs to go back to school, permission slips, bag lunches, even show-and-tell items. This space might be a shelf in a closet, a box on a shelf, or a basket on a counter.

Student Backpacks and Coat Hangers

The students should have a space to keep their coats and backpacks in school. Teach students how to hang up their coats, stuffing mittens and hats inside the sleeves. Have the students' spaces organized in alphabetical order and labeled with their names. If they do not have lockers, you may want to provide a cardboard box to place above their coats so that they can store their personal items such as gym shoes, etc.

Managing Time

Students need to learn to manage their own time. Adults in their lives so often tell them the time (or what it is time for) that they never learn how to budget their own time. One suggestion is to have a period of time each day for the children to accomplish certain tasks. Allow them to choose how much time to spend on each task so that they learn to budget their time. List the expectations on the chalkboard, such as in this example for a reading class.

1. Read the story on pages 12–40.
2. Answer the questions on page 41.
3. Work on the writing project.
4. Free read.

Let students know that they have an hour for the above tasks and that they need to budget their time. Go through an example. Talk about priorities—which of the above tasks are due first, second, third, etc. Discuss time limits. Discuss open-ended tasks, such as the free reading, which might be done last.

Teaching Students to Be Organized (cont.)

Managing Time (cont.)

From the previous activity on page 21, the students can learn in which order to do the tasks and how to prioritize. Make your expectations clear, starting with when the tangible tasks are due. And then assist the students with advice as they learn how to budget their time.

For the first few sessions, help students budget their time by reminding them with hints such as these:

- *"Half of the class is over. Think about what you were hoping to accomplish today and re-evaluate your schedule."*

- *"There are 15 minutes left in the class."*

Once students learn to budget their time, they will spend much less time socializing at the wrong times and more time concentrating on their work and accomplishing a great deal. It is always more effective to have people take ownership in the actual process of learning.

It is also valuable to give children suggestions as to how to manage their time at home. Teach them to break down the tasks at hand. For instance, if they have a set of lines to learn from a play, teach them to concentrate on the task for a short duration per day, every day, and they will accomplish the memorization more easily than trying to accomplish the task in one long session. This method can be used for spelling words and flashcards, too. Encourage students to evaluate what time of day they do their homework. Have them take into consideration factors such as whether they are hungry, too tired, or whether the time is right before a big event, etc. Have them choose a time when there are few distractions, they are the least tired, and they are not hungry or under stress. It is helpful to choose the same time every day and to designate a

time and a location for the work that needs to be done. This procedure can carry over into other aspects of their lives, such as practicing piano, doing chores, studying for religion classes, even playing with their friends. They might make it known that they are never available on Saturday mornings from 8:00 A.M.–10:00 A.M. Their friends won't tempt them with plans for those times, and they will be free to attend to their tasks.

Teaching children to manage their time is essential—not only for you to have an organized classroom but also for students to gain the most from their academic careers.

Beginning of the School Year

The time you spend setting up your classroom at the beginning of the year is important. For not only are you preparing for the arrival of your students, you are also preparing yourself for an entire year of teaching. You need to begin with an organized classroom which has set routines—a classroom that will be run in an educational, enjoyable, yet orderly fashion.

Setting Up Your Classroom

Your classroom must be set up so that it is functional, organized, and a pleasant learning environment for from the students. Refer to the first chapter, Setting Up Your Classroom, for suggestions as to how to attain this.

Gathering Supplies

Depending upon the setup of your school district, you may be given supplies, you may go select them the school's supply storage, or you may need to go out and purchase supplies yourself.

Once you gather your supplies, don't hesitate in putting them away. Find locations that are convenient and logical. Don't store all of your supplies in a big box in your closet and think that you will easily be able to access them later. Don't throw them all into your desk to arrange later. Store and arrange them *now* in an organized way. The following list will be helpful in getting started. You may need to add to or delete from the list, depending upon your needs.

- several sharpened pencils
- an electric pencil sharpener (saves time)
- blue, black, and red ink pens
- erasers
- permanent markers–wide and thin tipped
- overhead projector markers
- markers for children's use
- pencils and pens for students' use
- container for students' supplies
- manual pencil sharpener for young students
- mini-mailbox for correspondence with students (See Creating Order in the Classroom, page 14.)
- lesson plan book
- file folders
- daily task book
- meetings book
- student information book
- parent communications form
- substitute plan pages
- resource books for your teaching
- chalk

- erasers
- tacks
- tape
- stapler and staples
- bulletin board
- classroom posters
- first-day rules poster
- name tags for kids
- blank paper
- notepaper
- stationery
- recordkeeping book
- chapter books to read to the class
- storage baskets for various items
- in/out basket
- first-aid kit, including latex gloves
- attendance slips
- lunch slips
- stickers and stamps
- progress reports
- various colors of carpet samples

Beginning of the School Year (cont.)

Making Lists

At the beginning of the year, it is important to keep a running list of items that need to be completed. Make a master copy and duplicate it to use each year. Store it in a file labeled "Beginning of the Year." As each task or item is completed, check it off. Like the checklist used by all pilots (no matter how experienced they may be) before taking off, this procedure will prevent you from overlooking some important element of your preparation. The following is a list to be used; adapt it to your style.

Beginning of the Year

❏ Create student information book.

❏ Compile daily task list book.

❏ Compile meetings book.

❏ Compile substitute information.

❏ Obtain or select lesson plan book.

❏ Obtain or select record book.

❏ Gather notepaper.

❏ Create current file system.

❏ Create seating charts.

❏ Gather chapter books to read to the class.

❏ Gather all supplies from previous list.

❏ Prepare first week of lesson plans.

❏ Gather materials for first week of lessons.

❏ Make name tags.

❏ Label desks.

❏ Label coat hangers.

❏ Have lunch count ready.

❏ Have attendance sheets ready.

❏ Have emergency drill posters ready.

❏ Have first-day rules poster made.

❏ Have stickers and stamps organized.

❏ Have progress reports gathered.

❏ Review students' records.

❏ Have music ready.

❏ Place schedule on board.

❏ Have chalkboard organized.

❏ Have classroom books organized and labeled.

❏ Have teacher desk arranged.

❏ Have classroom desks arranged.

❏ Have teaching area set.

❏ Attend initial meetings.

❏ Set up recordkeeping system.

❏ _____

❏ _____

❏ _____

Beginning of the School Year (cont.)

Completing Tasks

It is essential that you prioritize your beginning-of-the-year tasks and complete them prior to the first day the students arrive. You must begin the year organized and with the very good intention that you will remain organized throughout the year. Don't procrastinate. If you look down your list and come to an item that you don't feel up to doing, do it now and get it over with or cross it off your list altogether. If it is worth doing, it is worth doing now, and then it is done. If the item is important and you feel you will have more time a few weeks after school has begun, place it later in your schedule. Plan such items sparingly. Feel good about completion; place a check mark next to every task you complete. If you complete a task that wasn't on your list, write it down just to feel the sense of accomplishment as you check it off. It is very rewarding at the end of the day to see a list a page long with check marks or pluses running down the length of the list. Reward yourself for your accomplishments.

At the beginning of the school year before the students arrive, allow yourself enough time to set up your classroom. You should have time set aside so that you can go through your materials, supplies, old files, and new mail. Make sure your energy level is high so that you put effort into the classroom setup. If you are tired and drained, you will resort to making piles instead of files. Once you have an organized classroom, you will be ready to take on the roomful of eager learners!

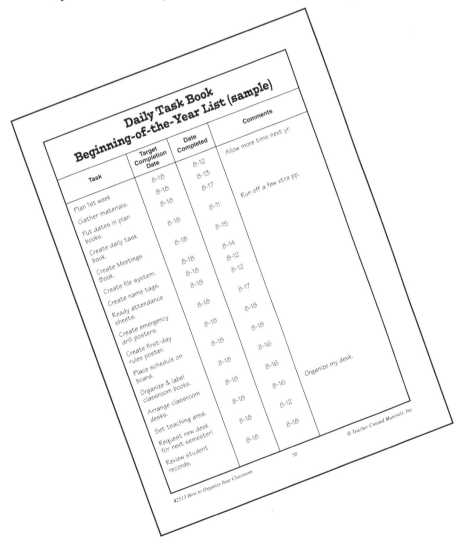

Daily Task Book
Beginning-of-the-Year List (sample)

Task	Target Completion Date	Date Completed	Comments
Plan 1st week.	8-18	8-12	Allow more time next yr.
Gather materials.	8-18	8-13	
Put dates in plan books.	8-18	8-17	Run off a few xtra pp.
Create daily task book.	8-18	8-11	
Create Meetings Book.	8-18	8-15	
Create file system.	8-18	8-14	
Create name tags.	8-18	8-12	
Ready attendance sheets.	8-18	8-12	
Create emergency drill posters.	8-18	8-17	
Create first-day rules poster.	8-18	8-18	
Place schedule on board.	8-18	8-18	
Organize & label classroom books.	8-18	8-16	
Arrange classroom desks.	8-18	8-16	Organize my desk.
Set teaching area.	8-18	8-16	
Request new desk for next semester!	8-18	8-12	
Review student records.	8-18	8-18	

58

End of the School Year

The end of the school year will either sneak up on you, or you will be counting down the days until you wave your final goodbye to the students. Either way, the end of the school year means an effort towards organization and preparation so that the transition to the next fall will happen smoothly.

Packing Things Away

Begin packing things away when you know you are finished using them. This process may begin as soon as the first few weeks of school have gone by. If you are through with the unit "My First Day of School," pack it away until next year. Think about each item you use each day. If you no longer have a use for it and can't foresee using it during the remainder of the academic year, pack it. It will leave more room for more important items in your classroom.

Making Lists

Make another list, this time labeled "End of the Year," and create a file for it. Run copies of this list to use at the end of each school year. Place a check mark near each item that you complete. You may want to indicate the completion date next to it. Always save this list for reference. Store it in your "End of the Year" file. An example of the end-of-the-school-year list follows, to be adapted to your needs.

- _____ Hand out all papers.
- _____ Finish recordkeeping.
- _____ Complete report cards.
- _____ Follow up on all parent communications.
- _____ Pack away all posters.
- _____ Pack away all supplies.
- _____ Pack away all resources.
- _____ Wash boards.
- _____ Clean out student desks.
- _____ Plan lessons for the first week of school in the fall.
- _____ Gather materials for the first week of school in the fall.
- _____ Go through all mail and magazines.
- _____ File all papers.
- _____ Go through old files and clean them out.
- _____
- _____

End of the School Year *(cont.)*

Preparing for Next Year

Although you will always spend time in the fall to prepare for the beginning of the year, it is important to get somewhat organized at the end of the year so that the transition is smooth.

1. Take some time to decide what areas you will begin teaching next year.
2. Pull the files, and take them home to begin planning lessons.
3. Have the first week of lessons planned, as well as the materials prepared, if you are certain what you will be covering that first week.
4. Familiarize yourself with the titles and contents of resource books that you will be using next fall.
5. Read books during the summer that you will be using in your lessons.
6. Organize and clean out your files at the end of the year when everything is still fresh and you remember what you needed and what you didn't need.
7. Pack away students' records so that you will have room for the upcoming class list of information.
8. Make up your new lesson plan book or obtain a new one.
9. Compile the Daily Task Book and pull out the Beginning-of-the-Year List. Begin checking things off that you complete that are on both lists.
10. Look ahead at the Beginning-of-the-Year List and complete anything that you have time to complete now.

Storage

Storage is important if you are moving from one classroom to another. If you remain in one classroom from year to year, storing your materials is essential if others use your classroom during the summer or if you are concerned with the dust that might attach to your materials. Whatever your needs are, make sure you begin saving boxes by requesting that the custodian save them for you at the beginning of the year so that by the end of the year you will have your boxes ready for storage. Make sure to label the boxes clearly with your name, your room, and the contents of the box. Organize the items in the boxes logically—supplies in one box, books in another, etc. Resist the temptation to throw everything into one box—it will take much longer to sort through when you are unpacking.

Although the temptation is great at the end of the year to walk away from the loose ends, leave time and energy to wrap things up in an organized manner. Time spent packing, planning, cleaning, and looking ahead will save time in the future, and it will allow you the self-satisfaction (not to speak of the relief!) of knowing that you will be coming back to an organized classroom in the fall.

Time Management

It is essential for you to learn how to manage your time. Time management is by far one of the most crucial points of the whole system. You must realize that your time is valuable. You must respect your time and work very hard every day to use all of your time wisely.

Seconds and Minutes Count

When you arrive at school, realize that your job and day have begun. You need to get down to business immediately. Don't be anti-social, but do be disciplined. Look at your goals and priorities. If your goals are to be an outstanding teacher, to be organized, and to have time left over for your family, then strive toward that and do that! Get your work—at least some of it— done during the day. The following steps will help you learn how to use every minute, indeed every second, to its full capacity. Taking these steps will enable you to use the often-wasted time for something productive.

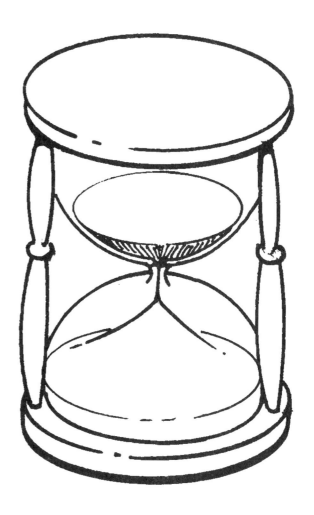

Always remember, however, that your first priority is the students. Be skilled enough at doing little tasks that you are still fully available to the students at all times. Don't get so engrossed with a task—such as correcting spelling tests, for example—that you miss the opportunity to observe or interact with the students as they are standing in the lunch line. If you are using the time during recess to correct tests, yet you have a student who is worried about an assignment, make sure you make time for the student. Students are your first priority!

- Use the few minutes it takes the students to wash their hands before lunch to correct something (such as the spelling tests) or to go through your mail.

- Use the few minutes it takes for kids to move from one class to the next to jot down notes about a student.

- Use the time before a meeting begins to update your task list, write notes, review lesson plans, or correct papers. (Be organized enough before a meeting to gather the work to bring to the meeting.)

- Use the time you are supervising children (if it is appropriate, such as during a video or TV program) to correct papers or review work.

- Use the time after school when the children have left to follow up on business.

- Use the time during recess to get something substantial completed.

- Use the time when children are coming in from recess to get your mail or go through your mail.

Time Management *(cont.)*

Seconds and Minutes Count *(cont.)*

Each of these "moments" adds up to a substantial amount of time that can be spent completing various important tasks throughout the day. Learn to recognize the importance of each second. Soon you will be using your time well, and you will find that at least sometimes at the end of the day you can go home with an empty school bag. Whether you are spending these little moments interacting with students, observing them, or accomplishing tasks, you will begin to appreciate the value of time.

Stay Organized

Once you have your whole organizational system in place, it is important that you maintain it as if it were the health of your classroom. You must exercise the system, feed it, tend to it, and actually love it. You must believe in it for it to work. And then it will. Always make sure you have a chance at the beginning of the day, during the day, or at the end of the day for simple maintenance:

- Move classroom furniture back in its place.

- Keep chalkboard information up to date.

- Make sure calendars are up to date.

- Make sure you are caught up with correcting.

- Make sure you are caught up with recordkeeping.

- Make sure you are ahead on lesson planning.

- Make certain you are prepared with lesson plan materials gathered.

- Make certain you are completing all daily tasks.

- Check to make sure you have a minimum in your "immediate business file."

- Make sure you have no mail in your mail pile at the end of your day.

- Make sure you are updated on parent communication.

- Make certain your files are organized and you haven't stuffed unwanted papers into your files.

Keeping the above tasks up to date and maintained will keep you organized, proficient, and stress free. If you notice that you have overlooked any of the above, such as falling behind in reading your mail, plan a time during the day to complete it; write it down as a task, and follow through to complete that task.

Time Management *(cont.)*

Set Goals and Priorities

Goals and priorities are oftentimes overlooked in the daily schedule of the academic teacher simply because teachers usually think that the goals are self-evident:

- to be a good teacher,
- to plan accordingly,
- to teach well.

Although these goals are the most worthy to mention, it is important to really write down specific goals and priorities. Begin with the priorities:

1. Take some time to think about what is important to you in your life (list big categories: religion, family, teaching, health, financial security, etc.).
2. Rank these priorities in order of the most important to least important.
3. Now, write down the goals you would like to meet under each heading; be specific and realistic but don't underestimate your ability to achieve. (For example, you might write "spend more time with my family by not bringing school work home on weekends.")
4. Finally, focus in on the goals you set for your teaching. Make a copy of them and place that copy on your desk. It is important to keep a copy of your master list of priorities and goals, as well, because your personal life reflects upon your professional life, and vice versa. You cannot meet conflicting goals, such as trying to spend more time planning at school and still spend more time at home. Your two lists of priorities must work together.

Now, write out a step-by-step program of how you will achieve these teaching goals (you can do it with your master list as well). Include dates or limits. For example, if one of your goals is to be an organized teacher, define for yourself what "organized" means. Then list your expectations:

- *"I will have corrected all papers by the time I leave school each day."*
- *"There will be no mail in my mail bin by lunchtime each day."*
- *"I will consistently have my planning done a week in advance."*
- *"I will spend three hours a week researching new teaching ideas."*

It is important to review these goals and priorities periodically to see if you are achieving them. You might even indicate this review on your daily task list every week or month as "check goals and priorities."

Actually writing down your priorities, goals, and the steps to achieve them will not only solidify your ideas but will also remind you to keep track and will help you to reach your expectations.

Time Management *(cont.)*

Meet Deadlines and Keep Appointments

It is obviously essential that you meet deadlines, be they deadlines set by your principal, by a parent, or of your own accord. You must respect deadlines and make no excuses to yourself for missing them. The following procedures will eliminate the missed deadlines and allow you to meet deadlines, as well as people's expectations.

1. Write down a date or deadline immediately upon notification. Don't delay! Write it down in your calendar the day it is due.

2. Write down the same deadline in your task list, far enough in advance so that you can prepare. (For example, on Tuesday, write *"Prepare for conference with Johnny's mom on Thursday."*)

3. In your daily task list, write down the day of an event and the actual appointment, stating *"Johnny's mom's conference prepared?"*

4. Purchase a mini-alarm. You can buy these the size of mini-calculators, and you may even find one the size of a credit card. Set the alarm to notify yourself of an appointment a few minutes in advance so that you have time to gather your materials and travel to the appointment spot. (Many teachers might choose not to have the alarm because they refer often enough to their task list and can keep a mental alarm in their heads. But for those who look down at the end of the day at their task list and find themselves saying, "Darn, I was supposed to call Johnny's mom today at 1:00 P.M. for a phone conference," the mechanical alarm will prove a welcome addition to their professional equipment.)

Keeping deadlines and appointments is one of the most crucial points to being organized. This is true not only because of the actual importance of the appointment or deadline but also because it shows respect, gains respect, and builds others' confidence in you as a professional.

Parent Communications

It is essential to maintain good communication between the parents and the school. With both of you on the same team, you can both strive towards the same goals for the child. If you begin the year on the right foot and gain the parents' respect and cooperation, your year will be easier when you look to the home for support with discipline concerns or academic problems.

To start out on the right foot, you may want to send an introductory note home, mentioning your name and your goals for the year. You may choose to invite the parents in to meet you before or after school on the first few days of school; or if your district calls for it, you may wait until the "open house" or "back-to-school night" when the whole school is open for parents to tour and meet the teachers.

Notes to Home

Whether it is a carefully composed letter or a brief note jotted down, any notes home should contain a few key elements:

1. Use a professional letterhead. If your school does not provide it, devise a letterhead and make copies of it. You may want to choose a color and use that same color throughout the year. At the top of the page, make sure your name and classroom as well as your direct phone number or the school number are included.

2. You may wish to use headings such as those listed in the Master Copies section (pages 70 and 71) at the end of this book.

Calls to Home

It is important that you set up your Student Information/Parent Communications Book (master copies can be found on pages 52–57). This information book contains an area to record communications with parents. It is important to keep an accurate record of these communications.

When using the form, you need to include the date you call the parent, the time, and the exact correspondence as well as the mode (phone, left message, etc.) of communication.

When you receive written correspondence, indicate that in your book and code each (for example, "A" on both the letter and the entry in your book) and then place the written correspondence into a file marked "From and To Parents."

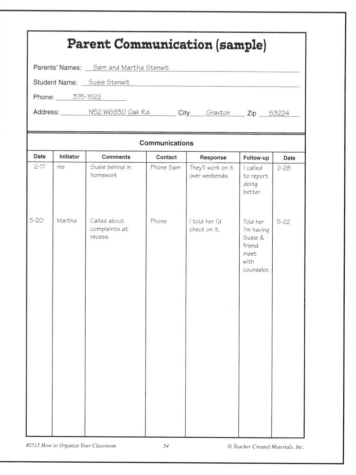

Parent Communication (sample)

Parents' Names: Sam and Martha Stenwit

Student Name: Susie Stenwit

Phone: 375-1522

Address: N52 W6930 Oak Rd.   City Gravton   Zip 53224

Communications

Date	Initiator	Comments	Contact	Response	Follow-up	Date
2-17	me	Susie behind in homework	Phone Sam	They'll work on it over weekends.	I called to report doing better.	2-28
5-20	Martha	Called about complaints at recess.	Phone	I told her I'd check on it.	Told her I'm having Susie & friend meet with counselor.	5-22

#2513 How to Organize Your Classroom   54   © *Teacher Created Materials, Inc.*

Parent Communication (cont.)

Calls from Home

When you receive a phone call, grab the Student Information/Parent Communications Book and take it to the phone with you. As you are talking, take notes, and make sure to enter the date, time, contact person, the correspondence, and any follow-up needed.

Finally, you should transfer needed follow-up into your daily book. Then don't forget, once you follow up, to include the results back into your communications book.

Notes from Home

When you receive a written correspondence, indicate it in your Student Information/Parent Communications Book, code each (for example, "A" on both the letter and the entry in your book), and then place the written correspondence into a file marked "Notes To and From Home."

Date the notes from home and save them for the year.

Direct Contact

When an individual makes direct contact, such as parents stopping by the classroom, indicate who initiated the direct contact, the date, time duration, and follow-up. Be specific as to what was covered.

E-mail Messages

Print a copy of e-mail messages and the responses; then file them in the correspondence folder. Follow up by noting the action needed in the Daily Task Book.

Voice Mail

Document all messages you receive or leave in voice mail and indicate them in your Student Information/Parent Communications Book. Record any follow-up messages in your Daily Task Book.

> **One of the most crucial aspects of your teaching is communicating successfully with parents. Keeping accurate records will enable you to maintain communications that will enhance your teaching.**

Organizing Mail, Messages, and Business

Mail, messages, and paperwork—these clutter up our days, our desks, and our minds. What can be done with the endless letters from book clubs, notes from parents, papers, and requests from principals, especially when you are trying to spend your time teaching? The following ideas and suggestions will help you to handle this office work so that you have time to teach.

Immediate Business and Mail

On your desk, make a special shelf or basket labeled "Immediate Business." Put anything in there that you receive but which you haven't yet dealt with. Make it your utmost priority NOT to put anything into this basket. Here is why: the more you have in that basket, the less important the items in it will seem to you. You will forget about the timely project that you have put there, and the pile will get bigger and bigger. Important things will get sifted to the bottom, lost under junk mail.

Instead, take new items—such as papers, letters, notes, mail, anything—into your hands when you have at least 20 seconds to deal with it! Don't retrieve your mail from your mailbox when your kids are ready to begin science class. Instead, get your mail when the kids are at recess. Then, take 20 seconds anytime you have something in your hand and make one of these three decisions:

1. Recycle	2. File	3. Immediate

Decide and act—NOW!

Don't look at a catalog and think that when you have time you will browse through it. You know you have no budget for ordering new classroom furniture, anyway. So toss it. (Or better yet, put it in the magazine bin for the kids to cut up!) Another similar catalog will arrive in one month anyway. If it is a note asking you to return a call, grab your Student Information/Parent Communications Book and call the parent back—now! Record your effort. File the note. Now it's done!

Do everything that you can whenever you have 20 seconds. Twenty seconds 45 times a day is a lot of time to accomplish things. Put things into the immediate business basket only if you really can't deal with it now, such as preparing a lengthy written response to a parent. Then put it in the "immediate business" and complete the task the first moment you have free. (Be sure that you write that task down on your task list!)

Never leave your classroom at the end of the day with something in your immediate business basket unless you indicate it on another day on your task list.

Organizing Mail, Messages, and Business (cont.)

Current Business

Current business (like book orders) that cannot be done on a certain day because you are waiting for all of the orders to be handed to you) can be placed in the "immediate business basket," but it would be better if you made a special place for those items. Immediate business is for priority mail that needs to be done in a timely manner.

For book orders, for example, get a strong magnet and a large envelope and store the orders in the envelope. Hang the envelope from the magnet on the inside leg space of your desk, hidden from curious little hands but just a grasp away from you. It won't clutter up your desk or the immediate business basket that should stay as clutter free as possible.

Messages

Whenever you receive a phone call, whether you are able to take it in your classroom or you need to go to a phone in the teacher's lounge or office, make sure you have your Student Information/Parent Communications Book with you in the event that it is a parent. Record details of the conversation in the book, and jot down any follow-up in your daily task list under "Priority." If the caller is not a parent, record the details of the conversation on your daily page in your Daily Task Book and record the item in your index. If you are unable to take the call immediately and you have a message on paper, don't rely on that piece of paper to remind you to make the call. Transfer the message onto your daily task list and discard the message paper. You will make the call when you notice it in your "priority" box. Use the same method even when you are initiating a call. You will then have an accurate record of your calls. Take your Daily Task Book and Student Information/Parent Communications Book to all calls.

Conferences and Report Cards

Conferences and report cards are periodic events and documents that need attention only at certain times of the year. Nevertheless, it is imperative that you organize your time, energies, and information so that when "that time" rolls around, you are well prepared and ready to complete the cards and hold the conferences. The first and most important step to this is keeping accurate daily notes.

Keeping Accurate Daily Notes

Keeping accurate daily notes is critical. Finding the time to record daily notes isn't difficult; remembering to do so is. To begin with, you will need to give yourself daily reminders in the Daily Task Book to "teach" yourself to use spare seconds to jot down notes. Once you get into the mindset of keeping daily notes, not only will you record information that will be invaluable when reporting time rolls around, but you will also enhance your observation skills by learning to be observant on an ongoing basis. In the Master Copies section (pages 51–96), you will find sample copies of how to keep accurate notes. Use one of these or several and tailor one to fit your needs. Take out the informational cards for a number of students (four, perhaps) per day. Don't put them away until you have recorded some information on each card. Then take out four new ones for tomorrow. Also make sure to jot down information that you think is pertinent for any child, even if you don't have that child's card out.

Recordkeeping

Recordkeeping is a task that every teacher must do. Here are some timesaving tips to make recordkeeping easier, more efficient, and accurate.

- When collecting tests to score and record, collect them in alphabetical order, last name first. You can then correct and record them straight down your chart, instead of taking time to find each name on the page to record the information.

- Use a pencil. You may need to change a grade, and a pencil keeps the page in better shape.

- Color-code using colored pencils. You might record daily assignments in blue pencil and test scores in red, for example.

- Always have your record cards on hand. This will allow you to record scores easily and efficiently.

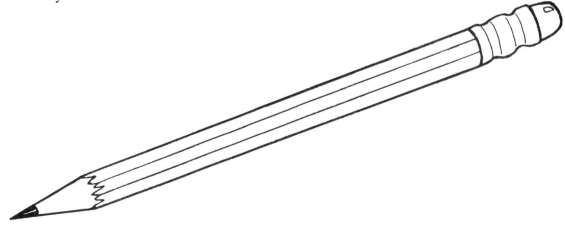

Conferences and Report Cards (cont.)

Arranging Your Room for Conferences

Every classroom is different, and everyone has his or her own style, so setting up for conferences is clearly a personal matter. Moreover, some teachers may feel that their everyday classroom is just fine to bring parents into. However, here are a few tips that could make a good impression on parents as well as create the right atmosphere for conferences.

- Leave the chairs off the desks. Have them pushed in, the room neat, and the desks in order.

- Clean the chalkboard. Have information written up on the board for the next day so that you can point out to parents how you display assignments, teach time management, etc.

- Make the conference area relaxing and inviting. You might have a vase of fresh flowers, a small lamp, or a dish of candy at the conference desk.

- Hang a sign on your classroom door with the schedule of conferences so that parents can double-check the conference schedule.

- Have a timer that rings if you have difficulty keeping to the conference schedule. It will remind you that the time has ended and will also notify parents that their time is up.

- Have classroom samples of student work, class books, or artwork for parents to look over while they are waiting to meet with you.

Being Prepared

Prepare well for each conference so that you are relaxed, well-informed, and ready for the questions that the parents may pose to you during the conference. Keep a sharp pencil on hand. The following tips will help you to be ready.

- Keep your parent communications cards, your recordkeeping, and your student information book on hand.

- Meet with each child's other teachers prior to the conference. Jot down any concerns they may have. Highlight those concerns that have appeared in more than one area.

- Go over each report card prior to each conference.

- Go over your student notes prior to conferences.

- Make notes of things you would like to cover at conferences.

- Make sure to keep accurate notes of conferences. Bring up the notes from the last conference. (*"Last time we talked about Johnny being reluctant to do his homework at home. How has that been going?"*)

Follow-Up

Immediately following each conference, before the next parent comes to your desk, jot down in your daily task book the follow-up tasks that need to be done. (For example, *"Check with Johnny's math teacher about homework assignments. Call mom back."*) Make sure to follow up and record this the next day.

Your File System

If you are fortunate enough to have plenty of file cabinet space to hold your files, clean them out to begin your new filing system. You will then have even more room for what is really needed, plus the extra space to make it not only an efficient way to gather materials but simple, too. You won't be jamming papers into folders and making your fingers sore with paper cuts. There will be plenty of room for filing. Throw away all those papers that you know are useless. Keep only those that are useful.

This project sounds simple, but it is tough. Here is the rule: *If you are unsure of the value of a paper, keep it for one year and discard it if you haven't glanced at it within the year.* Go through each file and each paper. Do this major project when you are refreshed and have plenty of time, such as a rainy day in the summer. Work on it a little at a time, or you may find yourself getting burned out and starting to save everything because you don't want to take the time to think about each item and make the decision.

Drawers

- Label the drawers to conform with the files that are contained within.

- Decide what to put into each drawer according to the proximity of the drawer to your work area. Don't put materials that you need at the end of each semester directly next to your desk. Use that space for the files you will be dipping into daily.

- Divide up your drawers by subjects. If you have four file drawers, use one for language and reading, one for math, one for science and social studies, and one for homeroom and business. "Business" is all of those things that fall into the business of teaching but aren't lessons—such as letterheads, award ideas, union information, etc.

- Within the drawers, make sections by subject as well as by level or area, such as "advanced" or "nouns and pronouns," etc.

- You should have one file area very accessible, possibly a file box to put near your desk, that you keep current information in. This would be a file for each of your current subjects as well as a file for correspondence (where you file notes sent to parents and received from parents) and other current business.

Your File System (cont.)

Subjects

Next, re-label the files themselves. Label them with titles that are relevant to your day. Look into the folder. Glance at the contents and think about what they are "about." The first thing that pops into your head is how you should label that file. Suppose that you have a lesson to file called "Mr. Round About" with a picture of a snowman on the front, and when you think of the lesson, a snowman pops into your head. You might then label the file, "Snowman—Mr. Round About" and file it under "S." The first thing that pops into your head now is probably the first thing that will pop into your head three months from now when you are trying to recall where you filed the lesson. In this way you will quickly be able to retrieve the lesson you filed.

Filing System

At the beginning of each drawer, you should have an information sheet, either on heavy tagboard and used as a marker or as a chart and stored in a file folder. On this form you should indicate the subject contents of all of the folders within the drawers—not necessarily the title of each folder. For instance, in your reading and language arts drawer you might indicate *"basal lessons," "trade books," "sentence lessons," "poetry,"* or *"plays."* None of the files themselves would be labeled as such; those subjects are too broad. But now you know what is within each drawer. Each title that you write on the sheet should be written with a colored marker, and the corresponding folder labels should be written in the same color. This will help you not only to quickly locate the folder but to replace it as well. As an example, I would write on my tag chart *"Trade Book Lessons"* (in blue marker), and then all of the files behind the "Trade Book Lessons" tag chart would be titles with specific headings written in blue.

Another option would be to have that same form but use it as a master form, not only for the drawer but also for the whole filing system. This will help you at a glance to know where to locate a folder. Color-code and number (by drawer) these as well. This option is particularly useful if you often have substitutes in your classroom and they would need to access files.

Upkeep

Finally, keep this system current and consistent. Once you have cleaned out your files, don't put anything useless into them. Make the decisive choice: *Recycle, File,* or *Immediate.* If it is *File,* it must be important. Put it in the right place and replace the folder. If it is a new entry, be sure you mark it on your master list. Although this might seem time consuming at first, soon you will have all areas clearly marked and indicated, and you will save valuable time by not having to search or make double file folders for the same types of content. Replace the files themselves in the correct spot. Keeping up with these small tasks will keep you organized and save you time in the long run.

Daily Task Book

The Daily Task Book will keep track of all of the tasks that you need to complete and items that you need to remember to do on a daily basis. It will also serve as a reference book to look back on. Refer to the related Master Copies pages (58–65) at the end of this book.

Daily Task Book Record Page

You should make copies of the daily record page to represent each day of the year. Fill out the specific date of each school day, including teacher workdays and days that you will be working in your classroom without the students. Fill out the dates all at once, not day by day. Unless you make it a habit to work in your classroom on weekends or holidays, you do not need to reserve pages for those.

Things to Do

Everything that needs to be done during your professional day, other than actual teaching, must be put on this list! Use the symbols to keep track of what you have completed, what you can delete, what you are plan forwarding, or what is in progress. Jot down all tasks that you do, even if you have already completed them. You will use this book as a reference to know that task has been taken care of and when. Take this booklet everywhere—to all meetings, phone calls, and planning methods. Jot down on the daily task list all things that need to be completed, such as papers that need to be corrected, students you need to talk to, people you need to meet with, and lessons that you need to plan. Don't ever leave any task to the mercy of your memory. Let this booklet do the work for you instead of trying to make mental lists. Any time something pops into your head that needs to be done, jot it down. If it is a task that doesn't have to be done today, jot it down on a day you know you might have extra time to work on that task. Plan ahead. For instance, if you know you need to contact parents in a few days with an update of their child's progress, page ahead five days and jot down a reminder.

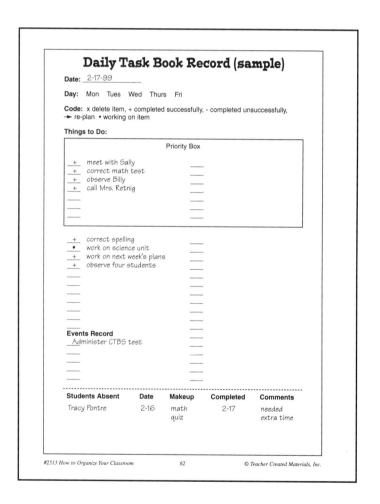

This booklet should be available to substitute teachers as well. The substitute should complete whatever he or she can during the day. When you return to the classroom, you will be able to note at a glance what tasks you still need to do to catch up and what has been done. You won't have to page through piles of papers left by the substitute and wonder what was completed.

40

Daily Task Book (cont.)

You should check your daily task list in the morning, during any free time throughout the day, and after school. You should never leave school with something on the list that you did not attend to. Indicate the standing of each item to be done by taking one of the following actions:

- Check it off with a *plus* because you have completed it, it was done well, or it was worth doing.
- Check it off with a *minus* if it was not done well or was not worth doing, but it was done.
- Put an *arrow* next to it and transfer it to another day
- Put an *"x"* next to it because you have deleted the task altogether, and it no longer needs to be dealt with at all.

It is important to visit each item on each list each day with a code so that you can tell at a glance what still needs to be done. It will also serve as an excellent reference that indicates what was taken care of and how it was done.

Priority Box

Although all of the items on your list are important to complete, there are a few tasks that must be done on a certain day at a certain time and cannot be planned forward. Examples of such items that would go into the priority box are these:

- *"Call Mrs. Smith about the fight Johnny got into this morning."*
- *"Prepare for tomorrow's sub."*
- *"Keep Sally in for recess to talk with her about the test."*

Items to go on the regular task list would be *"Work on the science unit,"* *"Correct math papers,"* etc. Even though the "regular" tasks are important, if need be they really could be dealt with the following morning. The items in the priority box must and will be dealt with within the day. Make time for them!

Students Absent

This is a place to indicate the students absent each day and what you need to do when they return. For example, you may need a reminder to hand a student a field trip permission slip on the day that he or she returns to school. Look ahead to the next day to record the student who was absent and the day on which he or she was absent. If that student is absent again, you need to forward the notation to the next day, and so on. For example, if Kevin is absent on Monday, you would write *"Kevin"* down on the Tuesday grid with Monday's date and the work he missed from Monday. Then Tuesday morning, when Kevin comes to school and you are reviewing your task list, you will notice that you need to hand him the field trip permission slip. You will hand him the permission slip and will have a record of doing so because you will immediately put a "plus" sign next to the task.

Daily Task Book (cont.)

Events Record

Use this area to indicate some event that you might later wish to refer to. For instance, you might jot down *"Received my contract to renew today."* The following year you will be able to refer to this page and know when to expect the contract that year.

Monthly Index

Create an index (pages 60 and 61) for each month, place it at the beginning of each month, and tab it for easy reference. Any task or event that you feel you will need to refer to at some later point, you should list on this page and then date it. Suppose, for example, that on December 1 you called a book club and ordered some books. They told you that the books would arrive in two weeks or you would receive a discount. The person with whom you talked at the book company was "Scott." On your task list for 12/1 you wrote down the details of the conversation, listing Scott's name and the discount.

You turned to your index and jotted down *"Book order, 12/1."* Then you turned to the promised delivery date and wrote on your task list *"Books should arrive."* Two weeks later as you are reading your task list, you notice that the books should have arrived and did not; so you check your index, which indicates a reference of 12/1. You turn to that page (12/1), read over your notes, and call Scott. You remind him of your conversation of 12/1 and the details of it, which included entitling you to the discount. You then record this transaction.

Any time there is something that must be done, write it down. You may need to know when you did it and if you did it. If you turn to the Daily Task Book Record, see it listed, and see that you checked it off (e.g., mailed in the book order), then you know it was done. The index helps you to locate a specific item in a more timely fashion.

This task book is essential for the organized teacher. It allows the teacher to keep track of important information, tasks, and events and encourages the teacher to complete tasks in an organized, timely manner.

Daily Task Book Index (sample)

Month of _____

Date	Item	Corresponds with/Date	Comment
2-12-99	Book order	3-10	Phone conversation w/ rep.
2-15-99	Ideas	2-15	Science unit ideas
2-28-99	Field trip	2-28	Notes on follow-up plans

Monthly Notes to Self:

February is a great time to order books—kids need them for spring break.

Meetings Book

This book is designed for you to keep track of the notes and minutes of all of the meetings that you attend throughout the year.

Make copies of the Meetings Book page in the Master Copies section (page 67). Then tab sections, indicating on the tabs the types of meeting you will be attending throughout the year, such as *district meetings, school meetings, unit meetings, curriculum meetings, social committee meetings,* etc. Reserve a section for workshops and conferences that you attend.

Crucial Points

When taking notes, indicate with a star or highlighter pen the crucial points of the meeting. Later, when you refer to your meeting notes, you can scan down to read the most crucial points first.

Notes to Self

Write down any thoughts or ideas that you would like to record that relate to any meetings you are attending.

Take this book along with you and write the notes from any meeting or class in the appropriate section, making sure you fill out the sections on date, day, and members present. Take it to all meetings, as well as to conferences and workshops that you attend. You will find that having the notes to all your meetings in one location will be helpful and efficient.

Student Information/Parent Communications Book

The Student Information/Parent Communications Book will be made up of a form for each student whom you teach. At the beginning of the year, you need to take some time and fill out the information needed (see pages 52–55).

Indicate the student's name on a tab, last name first, in alphabetical order.

Student

It is important to find out the full name of each student and also the name the student prefers to be called. This may turn out to be his or her second name or a nickname.

Classes with Me

Indicate what class or classes you have the child for. It will help refresh your memory when you are speaking to parents, especially at the beginning of the year when you are just learning names. You might want to highlight in color the tops of the cards according to what class you have the students in so that you can tell at a glance, using two colors if the student is in two of your classes. For example, for all of the students in your science class, highlight the tops of the pages in yellow. For those in your math class, highlight in green. For those few students who are in both your science and math classes, highlight in yellow and green.

Parents' Names

A student could potentially have four parents, some with last names different from the student's. This section will help you keep the names clear so that you can address them by the correct names when you come into contact with them or when addressing notes home to them.

Comments About Student

Use this area to record anything you need to remember about the student. During the year, make little notes that will help you assess the students and fill out report cards, watch for growth, or note areas of concern.

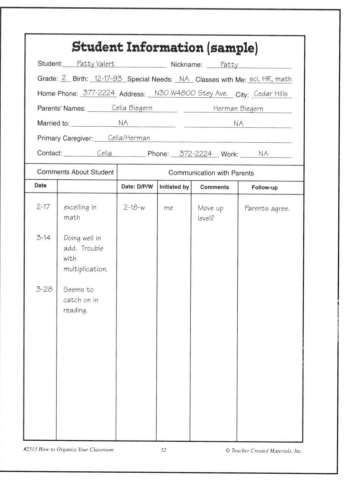

Student Information/Parent Communications Book (cont.)

Communication with Parents

This area is designed to record any interaction you have with parents. It can be kept separate as a self-contained book or used within this book. Use the form you feel will benefit you the most. The back page is blank to continue any notes that you do not fit onto the first page. You should review this area prior to conferences and when writing report cards.

It is nice to be able to follow up with parents on concerns that they had:

"We talked on the phone on the third of October about Tina's problem making friends. I have noticed that . . . ."

It is crucial to keep track of every communication that occurs with parents, filing copies of written correspondence as well. *Helpful Hint:* Anytime you are called out of the classroom for a phone call, grab this book. It is nice to have all needed information about a particular student on hand when his or her parent calls you. Then you won't be caught off guard. Indicate the date of contact and how the contact was made:

- **D** = direct (They stopped in.)
- **P** = phone
- **W** = written

Indicate who the contact was initiated by—the parent or you. Make sure you write down any follow-up actions that were taken.

Special Needs

Indicate any special needs of a child, such as the following:

- **LD** (learning disability)
- **ED** (emotional disability)
- **CD** (cognitive disability)
- **GT** (gifted and talented)
- **MED** (medical concern)

This information should also be located in the lesson plan book.

You will find the Student Information/Parent Communications book very beneficial. You will use it to document any concerns about a child, such as something the child said or did, a comment that you want to remember, any comment or communications from the parents or even other teachers and students. Use this book every time you are filling out report cards, writing notes home to parents, making groups for children, contacting parents via the phone, conferencing with parents, and discussing children with other teachers at staff meetings, team meetings, and meetings with the principal or the guidance counselor. The information will be crucial in following the development of each and every student that you are accountable for.

Substitute Plans

The substitute teacher section (pages 81–86) is meant to be partially completed and duplicated, and it should last the entire year. Once you have removed the original from this book and made copies, keep the lessons in one of the pocket folders in your plan book. Lay the lesson plans out on top of your lesson plan book on the morning a substitute teacher is to arrive. The substitute plans will help save you time and help the substitute closely follow the plans that you prepare. It will be beneficial to you, your substitute, and your students.

Information Letter

To begin, read over the information letter. Make several copies of it and store it in one of your pocket folders. When you are ready to write plans for a substitute, take one of these letters, fill out the date and the substitute's name, and write down any specific message at the bottom of the page under "Oh, one more thing." Messages you might include in this area are things that relate to the specific day or the specific substitute.

For example: *"If Johnny is in class today, please hand him the field trip permission slip to take home."*

Helpful Information Sheet

Next, fill out the helpful information sheet and then make several copies of it. This form is very important. Add information that would be particular to your situation, such as the procedures for hot lunch, etc.

Lesson Plan

Finally, fill out the lesson plan sheet. Indicate the times of the classes, as well as the subjects in the order that they are taught, starting from the top of the page. Draw parallel horizontal lines to indicate time periods. Don't forget to include periods such as attendance, lunch, and recess. Make several copies of this form prior to adding your lessons to it. Now staple one of each of the substitute pages together and store the substitute packets in one of the pocket folders in your plan book so you will always have them at your fingertips. When you need a substitute, all you need to do is transfer the modified lessons you want your substitute to use onto the appropriate page in your lesson plan book. Be sure to indicate in the appropriate areas where to locate materials needed to complete the lessons, as well as whether a lesson should be corrected, handed back to the students, or saved for you to review upon your return. The substitute will also have a space to indicate what portions of the lessons he or she completed. In addition, the form will encourage communication from the substitute teacher as to how the day went.

Substitute Plans (cont.)

Lesson Plan (cont.)

Leave your Daily Task Book open for the substitute. He or she can work on the things that you have indicated to do. Make sure to list things that are appropriate for a substitute teacher to do. Don't forget to include things like recess duty if you want your substitute to cover that during the day. If he or she does not check an item off, you know you will have to do it.

With a single glance, you will know when you are caught up with the day you missed.

When you return, file the used substitute form in a file folder titled "Substitute Used Form." You can then refer to this when planning for substitutes in the future. Before filing the form away, read the comments about the students and parents; then transfer any relevant notes into the communications book. For example, *"Bobby needed a field trip slip because he lost his"* does not need to be transferred. On the other hand, *"Bobby had a fight with Lee"* needs to be transferred with a note that it happened on the day you had a substitute teacher. Also, note the lesson the substitute had time to teach, and update your plan book accordingly.

The substitute section will be a quick and easy way to plan for a substitute. It will be helpful for the substitute because you will always have a consistent plan for him or her to follow. If other teachers in the district have adopted the system, the substitutes will look forward to going to those classrooms because of the consistent, clear, and organized lesson plan format that they are asked to follow.

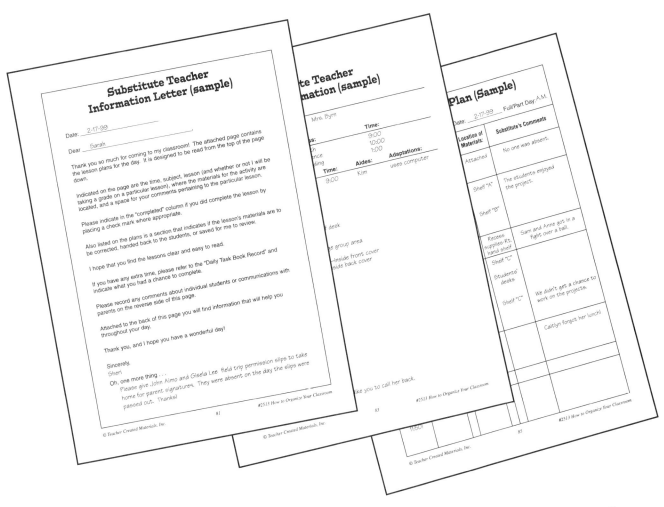

How to Set Up and Where to Begin

Now that you have this whole system in your hands, where do you begin? Begin by making the commitment to yourself that you are going to become a better, more effective teacher because you will make time to teach.

Read through this manual. Glance at the appropriate master copies as you are reading through the sections that mention them. Make sure to make one copy of all of the masters. Place them in a folder labeled "Master Copies" and keep the original masters with this book. You will then always have the originals for use in later years.

After reading through this manual, the next step is to set up for the school year.

Dates and Daily Task Book Record

Go to the Master Copies section (pages 51–96) of this book and select the master pages you need. Run off enough for the number of days you will be in the classroom, with or without students. Write the dates in the Daily Task Book Record pages. Make sure to take the time now to fill out the dates for the whole year instead of writing them in daily or weekly. You need to be able to page ahead (even several months) for planning, and it is inefficient to page ahead and not have the dates written in for your reference.

Run off enough copies of the Daily Task Book Record page for the whole school year, and date each page as stated above. Run off an index for each month of the year. Label the months with colored tabs. It should be set up as follows: August index, followed by a page of the daily task list for each day in August; September index, followed by a page for each day in September, and so on.

Place these pages in a notebook or bind them into a book. You can use a three-ring binder or bind them in combs. You can enlarge or shrink the pages before running them, depending upon how large you like to write and how big you would like the book to be. Keep in mind that this book should really go everywhere with you—your classroom, meetings, or home whenever you take classroom work home. So think about transporting and storing it when you are considering the size.

Substitute Teacher Information

Fill out as much of the substitute form as possible and then make copies. Put several of the copies in one of the pocket folders in your plan book (if you have pocket folders), or file them in a file folder labeled "Substitute Lesson Plans." Put the extras in a file folder titled "Master Copies" and place that in the "current" file box on your desk.

How to Set Up and Where to Begin (cont.)

Meetings Book

Make copies of the meetings pages that you feel will best suit your needs. Place them in a three-ring binder, staple them together down the left side, or spiral-bind them. Insert colored tabs and label them according to the meetings you will be attending throughout the year. Make sure you leave enough pages for each category.

Seating Chart

Make several copies of the seating chart (page 80). Laminate them. Laminate the "desks" page. Cut out the "desks" and use rubber cement to place them in the arrangement you would like. Rubber cement can be rubbed off when you need to reapply the desks in a new arrangement. You can fill out the "desks" on the seating chart with the students' names. Use permanent marker. When you want to erase the marker, spray it with hair spray and wipe immediately. Refer to the section on Setting Up Your Classroom (page 5) when creating the seating chart. You can also use tape, sticky notes, or simply write on the laminated paper with marker as alternate ways to arrange the seating on your seating chart.

Student Information Sheets

Choose the formatted student information sheet (pages 53 or 57) that will best fit your needs. Make enough copies for each one of your students.

Once you have made the copies, secure them into a book or binder of some sort, such as a three-ring binder—something that will be easy to open quickly and write in. You should avoid flimsy covers because it is best to be able to use the covers as a writing surface should you carry the student information book around the classroom and jot notes as you observe.

You may prefer to make copies of the pages on tagboard. This heavy tag will act as cards that you can tape along the top edges and then flip over to view the next card beneath it. Or, you can reverse the method and place the tape at the bottom and flip the cards down. Either way, the cards are heavy and will withstand the year's handling, and the flip method is fast and efficient.

Write the students' names on the cards. Fill in as much information as possible. Highlight the edge of each card through color-coding which class each student is in. Make sure to alphabetize the cards.

Make a book that contains enough cards for the students in one class (one per subject). Make a book for each class. Keep them on hand during each class and use them often.

You may take a copy of your report card and attach it to the inside cover of your student information book. This will help to remind you of the areas you need to be making comments on.

How to Set Up and Where to Begin (cont.)

Letterhead, Notes, Routing Forms, Request Forms

When time is of the essence, it is important that you not have to spend time on trivial tasks that can be avoided by adopting organizational methods. The following points will not only save you time and make you more organized but will also give you a professional method of correspondence.

- If your school district does not have letterhead stationery for you to use, select the format of letterhead most appealing to you in the Master Copies section (pages 70 and 71) of this book and have copies run. Store them in an easy-to-reach location.

- Select a "notes home" format and have it run off, storing the copies in the same location as the letterhead.

- Select a routing format (pages 68 and 69) that you like, fill it out, make copies, and store it in the same location as the letterhead and notes.

- Select a request form (pages 72 and 73) and have it run off. Place some copies in the same location as the other forms, as well as some copies in your lesson plan book.

- It is a good idea to run off each type of note on a different color of paper so that it will be quicker for you to select the type you need when you have only seconds to grab the paper and jot down a note.

Office Supplies

Before the first day of school, gather office supplies. Arrange your classroom and materials as suggested in the previous chapters. Review the manual on the usage procedures.

Ready to Begin

You are ready to begin the year with a new outlook and attitude. No longer will you be bogged down with those important but time-consuming, nonteaching tasks. You will now have at your fingertips many time-management and organizations methods that will allow you time to teach!

Master Copies Table of Contents

Student Information (sample)

Student: __Patty Valert__ Nickname: __Patty__

Grade: _2_ Birth: _12-17-93_ Special Needs: _NA_ Classes with Me: _sci, HR, math_

Home Phone: _377-2224_ Address: __N30 W4800 Stey Ave.__ City: _Cedar Hills_

Parents' Names: _____Celia Biegern_____   _____Herman Biegern_____

Married to: _____NA_____   _____NA_____

Primary Caregiver: _____Celia/Herman_____

Contact: _____Celia_____ Phone: __372-2224__ Work: __NA__

Comments About Student		Communication with Parents			
Date		Date: D/P/W	Initiated by	Comments	Follow-up
2-17	excelling in math	2-18-w	me	Move up level?	Parents agree.
3-14	Doing well in addition. Trouble with multiplication.				
3-28	Seems to catch on in reading.				

Student Information

Student:_____ Nickname: _____

Grade: ___ Birth: _____Special Needs: _____ Classes with Me: _____

Home Phone: _____ Address: _____ City: _____

Parents' Names: _____ _____

Married to: _____ _____

Primary Caregiver: _____

Contact: _____ Phone: _____ Work: _____

Comments About Student		Communication with Parents			
Date		Date: D/P/W	Initiated by	Comments	Follow-up

Parent Communication (sample)

Parents' Names: _____Sam and Martha Stenwit_____

Student Name: _____Susie Stenwit_____

Phone: _____375-1522_____

Address: _____N52 W6930 Oak Rd._____ City_____Gravton_____ Zip _____53224_____

Communications

Date	Initiator	Comments	Contact	Response	Follow-up	Date
2-17	me	Susie behind in homework	Phone Sam	They'll work on it over weekends.	I called to report doing better.	2-28
5-20	Martha	Called about complaints at recess.	Phone	I told her I'd check on it.	Told her I'm having Susie & friend meet with counselor.	5-22

Parent Communication

Parents' Names: _____

Student Name: _____

Phone: _____

Address: _____ City_____ Zip _____

Communications

Date	Initiator	Comments	Contact	Response	Follow-up	Date

Student Information Flip Book (sample)

Student Name: Antre, Sam   Parents' Names: John & Elizabeth

Student Name: Scott, Bill   Parents' Names: Tracy

Student Name: Carz, Cindy   Parents' Names: Zora & Cameron

Student Name: Dooni, Janet   Parents' Names: Beth & Ben

Student Name: Edward, Tim   Parents' Names: Brian & Susie

Student Name: Figne, Joe   Parents' Names: Troy & Tina

Student Name: Gonz, Ann   Parents' Names: Donna & Glen

Phone: 372-5235

Address: N32 W56 Oak   City: Cedar Hills   Zip: 52146

Comments:

2-15   Ann seems to be adjusting to her new school well.

3-19   Ann enjoys the arts.

Student Information Flip Book

Student Name: Parents' Names:

Phone:

Address: City: Zip:

Comments:

- -

Student Name: Parents' Names:

Phone:

Address: City: Zip:

Comments:

- -

Student Name: Parents' Names:

Phone:

Address: City: Zip:

Comments:

Daily Task Book
Beginning-of-the-Year List (sample)

Task	Target Completion Date	Date Completed	Comments
Plan 1st week	8-18	8-12	Allow more time next yr.
Gather materials.	8-18	8-13	
Put dates in plan books.	8-18	8-17	
Create daily task book.	8-18	8-11	Run off a few xtra pp.
Create Meetings Book.	8-18	8-15	
Create file system.	8-18	8-14	
Create name tags.	8-18	8-12	
Ready attendance sheets.	8-18	8-12	
Create emergency drill posters.	8-18	8-17	
Create first-day rules poster.	8-18	8-18	
Place schedule on board.	8-18	8-18	
Organize & label classroom books.	8-18	8-16	
Arrange classroom desks.	8-18	8-16	
Set teaching area.	8-18	8-16	Organize my desk.
Request new desk for next semester!	8-18	8-12	
Review student records.	8-18	8-18	

Daily Task Book
Beginning-of-the-Year List

Task	Target Completion Date	Date Completed	Comments

Daily Task Book Index (sample)

Month of _____

Date	Item	Corresponds with/Date	Comment
2-12-99	Book order	3-10	Phone conversation w/ rep.
2-15-99	Ideas	2-15	Science unit ideas
2-28-99	Field trip	2-28	Notes on follow-up plans

Monthly Notes to Self:

February is a great time to order books—kids need them for spring break.

Daily Task Book Index

Month of _____

Date	Item	Corresponds with/Date	Comment

Monthly Notes to Self:

Daily Task Book Record (sample)

Date: 2-17-99

Day: Mon Tues Wed Thurs Fri

Code: x delete item, + completed successfully, - completed unsuccessfully,
➤ re-plan • working on item

Things to Do:

Priority Box

+	meet with Sally	___	
+	correct math test	___	
+	observe Billy	___	
+	call Mrs. Retnig	___	
___		___	
___		___	
___		___	

+	correct spelling	___	
•	work on science unit	___	
+	work on next week's plans	___	
+	observe four students	___	
___		___	
___		___	
___		___	
___		___	
___		___	
___		___	

Events Record

_Administer CTBS test

___	___
___	___
___	___
___	___

Students Absent	Date	Makeup	Completed	Comments
Tracy Pontre	2-16	math quiz	2-17	needed extra time

Daily Task Book Record

Date: ________________

Day: Mon Tues Wed Thurs Fri

Code: x delete item, + completed successfully, - completed unsuccessfully, ➛ re-plan • working on item

Things to Do:

Priority Box

____ ____
____ ____
____ ____
____ ____
____ ____
____ ____
____ ____

____ ____
____ ____
____ ____
____ ____
____ ____
____ ____
____ ____
____ ____
____ ____
____ ____
____ ____

Events Record

____ ____
____ ____
____ ____
____ ____
____ ____
____ ____

Students Absent	Date	Makeup	Completed	Comments

Daily Task Book
End-of-the-Year List (sample)

Task	Target Completion Date	Date Completed	Comments
✔ Take posters down.	6-5-99	6-5-99	
✔ Fill out report cards.	6-1-99	5-30-99	
✔ Gather plan book for next yr.	6-4-99	6-1-99	Need new version.
✔ Follow up all parent communication.	6-5-99	6-2-99	
✔ Flag Mrs. Smith's letter for reference the first week of fall.	6-5-99	6-5-99	
___ Pack away all supplies.			
✔ Clean all boards.	6-5-99	6-4-99	
✔ Go through all mail & magazines.	6-4-99	6-3-99	
✔ File all papers.	6-3-99	6-3-99	
✔ Clean out old files & discard!	6-5-99	6-5-99	
✔ Clean out student desks.	6-2-99	6-3-99	
✔ Plan lessons for first week of fall.	6-5-99	6-4-99	
✔ Gather material for first week of fall.	6-5-99	6-5-99	
___ Remember to get more construction paper!	6-5-99		
___			

Daily Task Book
End-of-the-Year List

Task	Target Completion Date	Date Completed	Comments
_____			
_____			
_____			
_____			
_____			
_____			
_____			
_____			
_____			
_____			
_____			
_____			
_____			

Meetings Book (sample)

Meeting of: _Science Curriculum Team_   Meeting Leader: _Mrs. Jare_

Title: _team leader_

Meeting Date: _2-17-99_   Day: Mon (Tues) Wed Thurs Fri

Members Present: _me, Mrs. Jare, Christy A., Julie_

_____

Time: _____8:30_____ to: _____8:55_____

Crucial Points:

Science curriculum will be rewritten by June.

Meetings every Tuesday.

Discussion of textbooks.

Went through discovery kits.

Notes to Self:

Ask Mary at next meeting if we'll be ordering new textbooks by June.

Meetings Book

Meeting of: _____ Meeting Leader: _____

Title: _____

Meeting Date: _____ Day: Mon Tues Wed Thurs Fri

Members Present: _____

_____

Time: _____ to: _____

Crucial Points

Notes to Self:

A Note from the Teacher (sample)

Dear <u>Mrs. Ortiz</u>,

Your son John has shown an interest in drama. I would like to meet with you to discuss enrichment activities. Would 1-22-99 at 3:40 p.m. be convenient for you?

Sincerely,
Mrs. Bestor

✔ Please sign and return.

_____ Response from Parent:

A Note from the Teacher

Dear _____,

Sincerely,

____ Please sign and return.

____ Response from Parent:

Letterhead (sample A)

Sheri Mabry Bestor

Cedar Hills Elementary School—Room 17

12345 East Westminster Drive

Bennington, Indiana 93456

Phone: (845) 123-4444   E-mail: sbestor@abc.com

Letterhead (sample B)

Mrs. Sheri M. Bestor

Cedar Hills School, Room 17

12345 Westminster Drive   Bennington, Indiana 93456

Phone: (845) 123-4444   E-mail: sbestor@abc.com

Request Form (sample)

Person Requesting: _____ Sheri _____ Today's Date: ___ 2-17-99 ___

Instruction Regarding the: ☒ attached ☐ original

Please darken copies. _____

_____

_____

_____

_____

_____

_____

_____

_____

_____

_____

✔ number of copies: [32]   ✔ back to back   ____ stapled   ____ clipped

✔ color: _____ light blue _____   due by: ___ 2-28 ___   copies to: ___ JB, KS ___

✔ return to: _____ SB _____

✔ completed by: _____ Nancy _____

comments:

_____

_____

_____

Request Form

Person Requesting: _____ Today's Date: _____

Instruction Regarding the: ☐ attached ☐ original

_____

_____

_____

_____

_____

_____

_____

_____

_____

_____

_____

_____ number of copies: ☐   _____ back to back   _____ stapled   _____ clipped

_____ color: _____ due by: _____ copies to: _____

_____ return to: _____

_____ completed by: _____

comments:

_____

_____

_____

_____

Routing Form (sample)

Please pass the: ☒ attached   ☐ following   Date: _____2-17-99_____

To: HB _____   MM _____

DK _____   KS _____

KB _____   CA _____

JB _____   JP _____

(Please initial and indicate the date when this routing reaches you. Note any appropriate reactions below.)

Comments:

Please let me know what you think of the attached article on blending whole language and phonics instruction.

From: _____SB_____   Return to: _____SB_____

Date due back: _____3-17-99_____

Reactions:

Routing Form

Please pass the: ☐ attached ☐ following   Date: _____

To: _____ _____   _____ _____

        _____ _____   _____ _____

        _____ _____   _____ _____

        _____ _____   _____ _____

Comments:

From: _____   Return to: _____

Date due back: _____

Reactions:

File Index (sample)

Language Arts Units
subject

File:

File:	Dated Entered:		Date Entered:
Sentence Structure	8-98		
Nouns	8-98		
Verbs	8-97		
Adjectives	8-95		
Pronouns	8-98		
Adverbs	8-98		

(Color code all file folders within the subject.)

(Copy this form onto heavy tag.)

File Index

subject

Date Entered:

File:

Dated Entered:

File:

Classroom Seating Chart "Desks"

Instructions: Laminate this page. Color-code boys' names in green and girls' names in red, and write the names in permanent marker on the square "desks." Cut out the "desks" and attach to the seating chart in appropriate places with rubber cement. As seating changes, these "desks" can be lifted and moved to the new positions.

Classroom Seating Chart (sample)

Marn, Mark	Mart, Beth	Paron, Caitlyn
Steven, Brant	Coburn, William	Garcia, Maria
		Connolly, Sarah

Frank, Marcia	Munoz, Eddie
Smith, Annie	Schultz, Inge

Nguyen, Thuy
Payne, Max
Aimo, John
Lee, Gisela

Forbes, Evan	Berg, Leah	Mayamura, Hiroshi

Classroom Seating Chart

Instructions: Laminate this page and place "desks" with names in appropriate positions.

Substitute Teacher
Information Letter (sample)

Date: _2-17-99_____

Dear _____Sarah_____,

Thank you so much for coming to my classroom! The attached page contains the lesson plans for the day. It is designed to be read from the top of the page down.

Indicated on the page are the time, subject, lesson (and whether or not I will be taking a grade on a particular lesson), where the materials for the activity are located, and a space for your comments pertaining to the particular lesson.

If you did complete the lesson, please indicate in the "completed" column by placing a check mark where appropriate.

Also listed on the plans is a section that indicates if the lesson's materials are to be corrected, handed back to the students, or saved for me to review.

I hope that you find the lessons clear and easy to read.

If you have any extra time, please refer to the "Daily Task Book Record" and indicate what you had a chance to complete.

Please record any comments about individual students or communications with parents on the reverse side of this page.

Attached to the back of this page you will find information that will help you throughout your day.

Thank you, and I hope you have a wonderful day!

Sincerely,
Sheri

Oh, one more thing . . .
Please give John Aimo and Gisela Lee field trip permission slips to take home for parent signatures. They were absent on the day the slips were passed out. Thanks!

Substitute Teacher
Information Letter

Date: _____

Dear _____,

Thank you so much for coming to my classroom! The attached page contains the lesson plans for the day. It is designed to be read from the top of the page down.

Indicated on the page are the time, subject, lesson (and whether or not I will be taking a grade on a particular lesson), where the materials for the activity are located, and a space for your comments pertaining to the particular lesson.

If you did complete the lesson, please indicate in the "completed" column by placing a check mark where appropriate.

Also listed on the plans is a section that indicates if the lesson's materials are to be corrected, handed back to the students, or saved for me to review.

I hope that you find the lessons clear and easy to read.

If you have any extra time, please refer to the "Daily Task Book Record" and indicate what you had a chance to complete.

Please record any comments about individual students or communications with parents on the reverse side of this page.

Attached to the back of this page you will find information that will help you throughout your day.

Thank you, and I hope you have a wonderful day!

Sincerely,

Oh, one more thing . . .

Substitute Teacher
Helpful Information (sample)

Helpful Teachers:

Mrs. Budessi   Mrs. Butler   Mrs. Byrn
Mrs. Smithe   Mrs. Budne

Helpful Students:

Helpful Students:	Class:	Time:
Whitne M.	math	9:00
Kaiti A.	science	10:00
Scott B.	reading	1:00

Special Needs Students:	Class:	Time:	Aides:	Adaptations:
Karolyn	math	9:00	Kim	uses computer

Location of Materials:

First Aid Kit: top desk drawer
Today's Lessons: attached
Daily Task Book Record: on right of desk
Stickers, Stamps: left desk drawer
Textbooks: behind desk
Consumables for the Day: near large group area
Manipulatives: shelf behind desk
Seating Chart: lesson plans book—inside front cover
Class Lists: lesson plans book—inside back cover
Good News Notes:

_____

_____

_____

Emergency Procedures:

Fire Drill: Go out south door.

Tornado Drill: Go to hallway.

Earthquake Drill: NA

Comments Regarding Students:

Annie went home sick.

Communications with Parents:

Mrs. Maybry called. She would like you to call her back.

Substitute Teacher
Helpful Information

Helpful Teachers:

Helpful Students: **Class:**   **Time:**

Special Needs Students: **Class:**   **Time:**   **Aides:**   **Adaptations:**

Location of Materials:

    First Aid Kit:
    Today's Lessons:
    Daily Task Book Record:
    Stickers, Stamps:
    Textbooks:
    Consumables for the Day:
    Manipulatives:
    Seating Chart:
    Class Lists:
    Good News Notes:

    _____

    _____

    _____

Emergency Procedures:
    Fire Drill:

    Tornado Drill:

    Earthquake Drill:

Comments Regarding Students:

Communications with Parents:

Substitute Lesson Plan (Sample)

Substitute Teacher: _____Sarah Chang_____ Date: ___2-17-99___ Full/Part Day: A.M.

Time	Subject	Completed	Lesson (*graded)	Correct	Save/Return	Location of Materials:	Substitute's Comments
9:00-9:15	Attendance-Homeroom		Take attendance Say Pledge			Attached	No one was absent.
9:20-10:00	L. Arts	✓ ✓ ✓	1. Go over nouns lesson, p. 12. 2. Do project. * 3. Free read.	✓	S	Shelf "A" Shelf "B"	The students enjoyed the project.
10:05-10:20	Recess		Please take duty.			Recess supplies-Rt. hand shelf	Sam and Anne got in a fight over a ball.
10:25-11:15	math	✓ ✓	1. Take quiz.* 2. Do questions 1–20, p. 22. 3. Work on group projects	✓ ✓	S R	Shelf "C" Students' desks Shelf "C"	We didn't get a chance to work on the projects.
11:20-11:50	Lunch recess	✓	Please take students to lunch. Collect tickets.				Caitlyn forgot her lunch!
12:00-1:00	Reading						
I'll return by 11:50!							

Substitute Lesson Plan

Substitute Teacher: _____ Date: _____ Full/Part Day: _____

Time	Subject	Completed	Lesson (*graded)	Correct	Save/Return	Location of Materials:	Substitute's Comments

Classroom Map (Sample A)

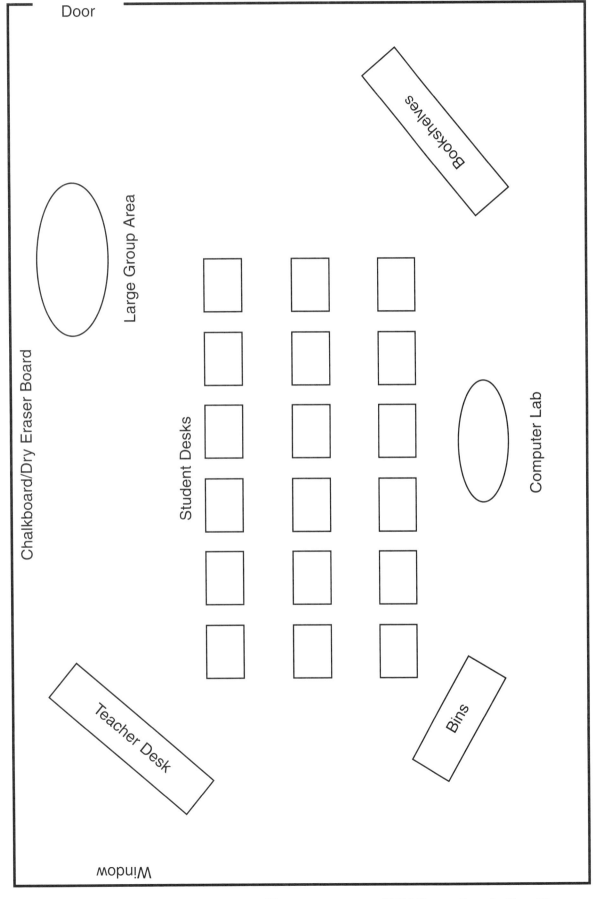

Door

Chalkboard/Dry Eraser Board

Large Group Area

Bookshelves

Student Desks

Computer Lab

Teacher Desk

Bins

Window

Classroom Map (Sample B)

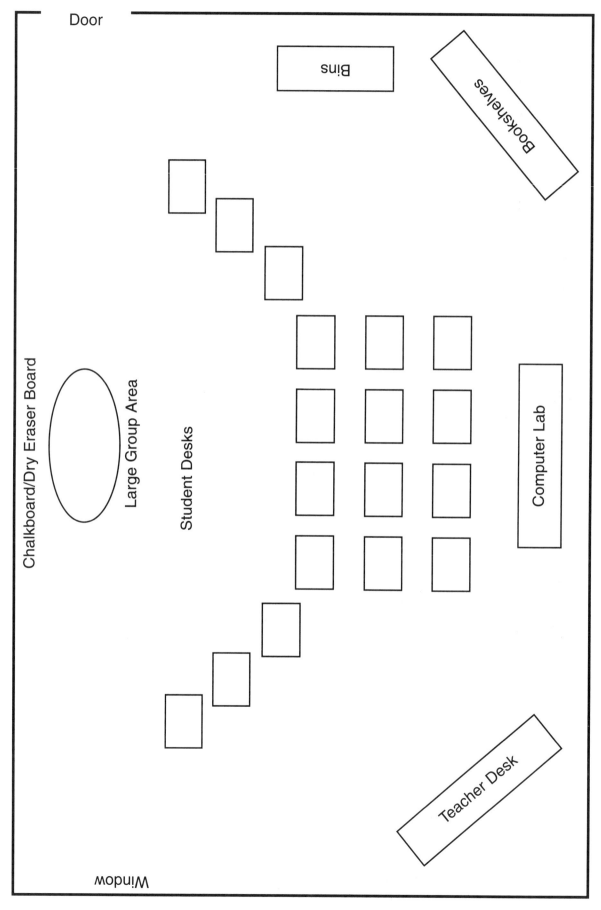

Door

Chalkboard/Dry Eraser Board

Large Group Area

Student Desks

Window

Bins

Bookshelves

Computer Lab

Teacher Desk

Chalkboard

Classroom Map (Sample C)

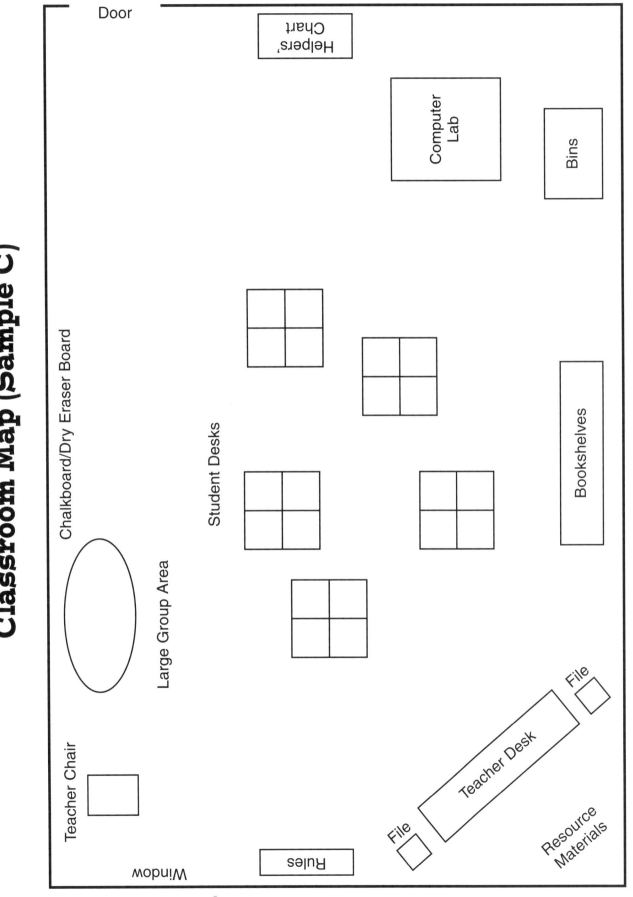

Door

Helpers' Chart

Computer Lab

Bins

Chalkboard/Dry Eraser Board

Student Desks

Bookshelves

Large Group Area

Teacher Chair

File

Teacher Desk

File

Window

Rules

File

Resource Materials

Book Checkout List

Teacher _____ Room _____

Subject _____

Name	Book	Date Checked Out	Date Checked In

Textbook Record Sheet

Text:	Publisher:	Date:

Book Numbers	Student Names	
	Comments:	
	Comments:	
	Comments:	
	Comments:	
	Comments:	
	Comments:	
	Comments:	
	Comments:	

Field Trip Checklist

Permission slips with parent phone numbers .... ☐

Food

    All student lunches with names .... ☐

    Every student with money for lunch .... ☐

    Cooler with ice and drinks .... ☐

Maps/Information Sheets .... ☐

Attendance .... ☐

Nonparticipants

    Put nonparticipant forms in teachers' boxes. .... ☐

    Gave materials to nonparticipants. .... ☐

Students understand rules on bus. .... ☐

Students understand field trip rules .... ☐

Student helpers to move lunches/cooler .... ☐

Special equipment/clothing .... ☐

Students understand what to bring. .... ☐

Keys/Wallet with extra cash .... ☐

Lock your door! .... ☐

Field Trip Letter to Parents

Field Trip Alert!

School_____

Date_____

Dear Parents,

Our class is planning a field trip soon.

Place: _____

Address: _____

Date: _____

The purpose of our activity is the following:_____

_____

Students will need the following: _____

_____

_____

_____

Teacher Signature

Please return this letter with your signature if you wish your child to participate in this activity.

_____has my permission to attend this activity.

_____

Signature of parent or guardian

Parent Conference Log

Student _____

Date _____

Parent(s) Present_____

Other Persons Present _____

Student's Positive Aspects

Concerns

Possible Solutions

Contract Needed?
Yes   No

Parent Volunteer Call

Date _____ Child _____ Class_____

Dear_____,

I am asking for volunteers to help in the following area(s):

_____.

The tasks would be to_____

_____.

              date(s)   time(s)

If you are interested in volunteering your time, please indicate your preference above. You will be receiving the bottom portion of this letter in return by _____ if I am able to use your help.

Thank you so much for your offer to help!

Sincerely,

- -

Parent _____ Child _____ Volunteer to help_____

on _____ from _____ to_____

_____Yes,_____, I would appreciate your help in volunteering for the dates and times below. Should you be unable to keep this commitment, please call me at_____at your earliest convenience. Thanks!

_____date(s)

_____time(s)

Parent Thank-You Letter

Date:_____

To:_____

From:_____

I just wanted to take some time to say "thanks" for your help recently.

It is parents like you who make our schools a great place to learn!

I can speak for everybody when I say you really made a quality difference. Don't just take it from me—here are the students: